The Boston Movement:
Critical Perspectives on
the International Churches of
Christ

Edited by
Carol Giambalvo
and
Herbert L. Rosedale

AN AFF BOOK

ISBN 0-931337-06-2

Library of Congress Catalog Card Number 95-080428

Printed in the United States of America

Contents

THE BOSTON MOVEMENT

Introduction

This book arose out of my experiences over the past few years in speaking with former members of various branches of the International Churches of Christ (sometimes more commonly known as the Boston movement). These individuals came to me, as many former cult members have, with claims of having been defrauded, deluded, and debased. They were going through the process of trying to rebuild their own sense of trust and self-confidence. Many were clearly idealistic, upwardly-mobile young adults who had spent a significant part of their early adulthood trying to establish themselves in society and staking out the goals they wanted to achieve and the ideals they wanted to live by. Now, after their experiences with the International Churches of Christ (ICC), they felt depressed, discouraged, and disillusioned.

All of this reminded me of earlier years when I had seen former cult members whose desires to create a better world of more loving communities and to battle the world's ills and assuage the pain of others had been sidetracked, abused, and exploited by various destructive organizations. But I also noted a difference with these former members of the Boston movement: in general, the people to whom I was now talking were not middle- or upper-middle-class white college students. Rather, they represented a multicultural spectrum as well as a number of people moving from sheltered and rural environments to a new urban environment, and people who had invested much of themselves in struggling to overcome the atmosphere of limited potential into which they were born. All, it seemed, had a firm belief in and commitment to self-achievement.

These new victims of cult exploitation projected a different identity within the population of former cult members, and reaching out to them was an important effort that had not previously been undertaken by those who provide postcult resources. So, I suggested to a group of these former members that they put together narratives that could reach their peers rather than rely on already-existing material designed for different targets of cultic recruitment. They were enthusiastic about participation in this project because they recognized the need for such communication. It was an exciting and inspiring experience for them to help create this book.

While reading the final product, I see the faces of the narrators shine out and perceive in their expressions their desire to help and warn others. I hear the pain between their words as they relate their experiences and relive their exploitation and abuse. I hope that readers of this book will find the common elements in the narrations that will lead them to understand how intelligent and sensitive people have been led to do things that they did not intend or want to do. I also hope readers will come to see how it is that circumstance and deception, rather than flawed elements of the persona, can lead people to join abusive and destructive movements.

The reader should keep two important points in mind while reading this book. First, members of the Boston movement, like members of other cultic groups, are simultaneously victims and victimizers. The distressed ex-members I have met were often psychologically abused by leaders who themselves may now be or may someday be distressed ex-members. Almost without exception the members and line leaders have good intentions. But they are caught up in a deceptive system which uses the enthusiasm of people desiring noble ends to justify unethical means of achieving ends that aren't so noble.

The second point to keep in mind is that even in powerful environments every person responds differently. Personality factors, family issues, social supports, practical circumstances, the character of a member's discipler—all of these, plus other variables, will affect how a person responds to a cultic environment. Some people are devastated. Some are deeply distressed; others mildly so. Some deny the distressing aspects of their cult experience and put it, so to speak, in a thermos bottle, which may spring a leak years after the person leaves the group. Thus, you will see considerable variation in the cases discussed in this book.

On the other hand, do not let the variety of individual responses blind you to the fact that cultic environments are indeed manipulative and exploitative. However much the group may profess love, when push comes to shove the group's goals and needs always come first. Members, as well as outsiders, are objects to be used, not subjects to be respected. That is why ex-members so often say they were psychologically or spiritually abused.

When many ex-members from a particular group independently report similar abuse, as do those who tell their stories in this book, outside observers begin to question the group's claims of benevolence. Books such as this one sometimes result from such questioning.

THE BOSTON MOVEMENT

Structure of the Book

This book is divided into four sections.

Part I provides background on the founding and growth of the International Churches of Christ (ICC). It includes a chapter by the Reverend Robert Thornburg who describes how Boston University, where he is dean of Marsh Chapel, managed to deal with complaints about the intrusiveness of ICC recruiters on campus. Thornburg's chapter includes the text of a booklet that was distributed on Boston University's campus in order to educate students and faculty about the ICC's methods.

Parts II and III are composed of a collection of personal accounts describing experiences with various branches of ICC. These firsthand accounts allow the reader to gain a better understanding of how people get involved with such groups and of the pressures brought to bear on recruits and members. We hope that readers will be able to identify with the questions, struggles, and issues raised by these young people.

Part II includes summarizations of four young adults' stories as told to Lorna and Bill Goldberg, two psychotherapists who specialize in working with former cult members. To protect the privacy of these individuals, we have used pseudonyms and changed some of the facts in these accounts. The Goldbergs' chapter, which leads off Part II, provides an overview of the common themes that emerge in working with former members of the Boston movement.

Part III contains three autobiographical accounts written by former ICC members, giving a somewhat fuller picture of their recruitment, involvement, and departure from the particular local group with which they were involved. This section concludes with an account by Kimberly Logan (a pseudonym), the mother of a young woman who joined and is still involved with the movement. We thought it important to include input from a parent, as it not only gives another perspective but also may provide solace and insight to thousands of parents around the country, and around the world, who no doubt struggle with many of the same issues as does this mother. Since ICC focuses its recruitment primarily on college campuses, many of its recruits have just recently left home. Most often, it is these new members' relationship with their parents that is the first to feel the negative impact of the person's involvement with the Boston movement.

Part IV contains two chapters by Carol Giambalvo, a leading exit counselor with considerable knowledge about the International Churches of Christ. She provides us with an insider's view of the exit counseling process as well as describing some of the analytical tools used in such meetings.

In Chapter 12, which is based on an actual case, Ms. Giambalvo describes the interchange that took place between an exit counseling team and a current member of an ICC church. The unfolding of the exit counseling sessions clarifies the issues involved as well as the process itself. ICC's questionable techniques are clearly revealed as Ms. Giambalvo takes us through the process of informing someone about the kind of deception and manipulation found in the group's recruitment activities and its ongoing efforts to gain and secure an increased commitment from members and recruits.

Both Chapters 12 and 13 show us the value of using the accepted criteria to define cultic environments as a means to evaluate a group's indoctrination practices and training techniques. In her exposition Ms. Giambalvo relies on Dr. Margaret Thaler Singer's six conditions for a thought-reform environment along with the eight psychological themes that

Dr. Robert Lifton associates with such environments. (Both sets of criteria are presented with commentary in the Appendices.) Clinical psychologist Margaret Singer is a leading authority on cults and psychological influence, and has made enormous contributions to this field during the past several decades.

In Chapter 13 Ms. Giambalvo focuses on Lifton's criteria as the guidepost for her analysis. As a researcher and professor of psychiatry, Lifton carried out a lengthy scientific study of the psychological influence techniques used in Communist China and during the Korean War. His seminal work, *Thought Reform and the Psychology of Totalism,* first published in 1961, gave the world one of the first in-depth looks at the interplay between ideology, identity, and human behavior.

For some years now, the eight psychological themes identified and described in detail by Lifton have been used by many as the criteria with which to measure whether or not an experience or group practice involves the use of thought-reform processes, thereby creating a cultic, or totalist, environment. Ms. Giambalvo's application of Singer's and Lifton's criteria, reinforced with examples from ICC's own writings as well as from the accounts told in this book, allows readers to measure the International Churches of Christ for themselves.

A final note of clarification: throughout this book the names International Churches of Christ (ICC), Boston movement, and Boston Church of Christ (BCC) are used interchangeably.

The International Churches of Christ came to the forefront of our attention rather recently. Just as quickly, it has become the subject of more telephone calls and communications to AFF and other cult-awareness organizations here and overseas than any other group at this time.

This book has been designed both to be a practical guide and to sound a warning signal. I truly hope that it will also be seen as a tribute to all of the former members of the Boston movement who contributed to it, since each of them regarded it as a reflection of personal travail as well as a celebration of overcoming a misstep along the road to self-realization.

Special thanks on this project go out to Bill and Lorna Goldberg who, because of their long-term experience and expertise, graciously took the time to help some of the individuals formalize their narratives. The Goldbergs also wrote an insightful overview of those meetings and their other work with former Boston movement members. Also, thanks to Janja Lalich for her sensitive editorial eye and her capacity to pull together the many parts of this project into a cohesive book. I also thank my coeditor Carol Giambalvo, without whose help this project never would have seen the light of day. And most important, both Carol and I wholeheartedly convey our appreciation to the following families for contributing financially to the production of this book: Dr. and Mrs. James Fitzpatrick, Dr. and Mrs. Jane Mahan, Mr. and Mrs. Stephen Reiner, Mr. and Mrs. Gary Sugg, and Mr. and Mrs. Robert Weber.

New York City
February 1996

Herbert L. Rosedale
President, AFF

Part I

An Historical Look
at the Boston Movement

1

A Brief History of the Boston Movement

Carol Giambalvo

The Boston movement grew out of the mainline Churches of Christ. It has its early roots in the ministry of Chuck Lucas, and first became known as the Crossroads Movement, named after the Crossroads Church of Christ in Gainesville, Florida.[1] It was there in 1967 that Lucas, while working as a campus minister at the University of Florida, began employing what are known as shepherding, or discipling, techniques.[2] Following the Crossroad Church's termination of Chuck Lucas in August 1985 for "recurring sins in his life," the leadership of the movement was taken over by Kip McKean, who, while a student at the University of Florida, had been baptized in 1972 by Lucas and trained in the discipling methodology.

The Discipling Methodology
The Boston movement is often referred to as the Discipling Movement because of its use of discipleship partners or discipleship groups. It is similar in nature to the practice described as shepherding in other groups. In 1984 McKean changed the terminology previously used in the Crossroads Movement from "prayer partner" to "discipling partner"; yet

the way the relationship worked was similar.[3] Today, the discipling partner is more often referred to as "discipler."

Discipling is hierarchical and pyramidal in nature, and in this movement, it refers to a system of intense training and supervision of new converts in order to raise them to a leadership position so that they can go out and "plant" new churches (or as they did in the early days, infiltrate local mainline churches) and recruit new disciples.

An authoritarian relationship exists between disciples and their disciplers who are placed "over them in the Lord." Disciples are taught to confess their sins to their discipler, to submit to and obey as well as imitate their discipler. The process of confession often is followed by rebuke, correction, and admonishment. All decisions are to be taken to the discipler for "advice." No area of a disciple's life is to be left uncovered or governed by personal decision making.

In each church the disciple-discipler relationship can be traced upward starting with the members to Bible Talk Leaders, House Church Leaders, Zone Leaders, Sector Leaders, then to the lead evangelist, and finally to World Sector Leaders, who are discipled by McKean. In practice, a member may be discipled by another member, who is discipled by an Assistant Bible Talk Leader, who is discipled by a Bible Talk Leader, who is discipled by a House Church Leader, who is discipled by a Zone Leader, who is discipled by a Sector Leader, who is discipled by an evangelist, who is discipled by the lead evangelist (in a church large enough to have more than one evangelist), who is discipled by the World Sector Leader, who is discipled by Kip McKean. McKean is discipled by no one, according to Al Baird, an elder in the Los Angeles branch of the church, a World Sector Leader in charge of Media and Law, and the former lead evangelist in the Boston church.

Significant Developments Within the Movement

After his college graduation in 1975, McKean left Gainesville and became a campus minister at Northeastern Christian Junior College, near Philadelphia. Ten months later he moved to Charleston, Illinois, having been hired by the Heritage Chapel Church of Christ as a campus minister to Eastern Illinois University, where he worked with Roger Lamb.[4] The intensity level of their ministry increased until eventually, in April 1977, the sponsoring church—the Memorial Church of Christ of Houston, Texas—fired both McKean and Lamb for the use of the discipling methodology.

This happened at a time when, throughout the country, the media began reporting mounting evidence of cultic practices and emotional manipulation by the movement. Concerns were being expressed about aggressive recruitment and the authoritarian one-over-one discipling relationship.[5] A series of articles in the local Gainesville newspaper in April 1979 explored charges that "tactics of manipulation and control were being used."[6]

Other media coverage nationwide cited the following allegations:

- The Crossroads ministry had become so elitist as to view itself as the only road to Christian salvation[7]
- Crossroads-trained ministers and converts were exerting undue evangelistic pressure on vulnerable students[8]

3

- There was financial pressure on members to contribute money and to procure loans to help finance the goals of the movement[9]
- Church policies were causing some young adults to forsake family and friends and to neglect study and job responsibilities in order to meet the requirements of membership[10]
- Some members were exhibiting personality changes, becoming more and more like their leaders[11]
- Members who left the movement were subject to harassment and/or shunning by former friends in the movement, resulting in psychological problems[12]
- Converts were assigned prayer partners to whom they must confess, and these confessions became common knowledge to leaders and other members and were used to maintain control of members[13]
- The doctrine instilled fear, guilt, and anxiety in some converts[14]
- Members were rebaptized or the movement withheld baptism on the basis of manmade judgments about converts' acceptability[15]
- The group employed mind control techniques[16]

In June 1979 McKean moved to the Lexington Church of Christ in Lexington, Massachusetts. Using the discipling methods, the church expanded rapidly from a membership of thirty. As church growth mounted, the congregation soon

4

outgrew the facility being used, and so renamed itself the Boston Church of Christ.

The Boston church became the seat of the movement. McKean improved on and embellished the practices of the Crossroads movement as he changed practices, jargon, doctrine, and strategies: for example, prayer partners became discipling partners, and Soul Talks became Bible Talks. The control tightened, and the hierarchical structure became more evident. McKean established House Churches, Zones, Sectors, World Sectors, Pillar Churches, Capitol City Churches, Small City Churches, and Countryside Churches. Churches that fell behind in baptisms were "reconstructed," their leaders recalled to Boston for "further training." Boston became the focal point of all training, and eventually leaders at the Boston-based church reconstructed churches previously known as Crossroads churches.

At a congregational meeting on June 26, 1988, the Crossroads Church of Christ in Gainesville, Florida, officially disassociated from the Boston Church of Christ Movement.[17] The elders cited concerns in the areas of the Boston movement's practice of usurping congregational autonomy, reconstructing churches, taking control of congregations, granting too much authority to leaders, and requiring that members obey their discipler in all matters (even in areas of opinion). Crossroads was also concerned with the changes in the structure of the movement, which had resulted in a stronger pyramidal structure with Boston as the Mother Church.

On June 24, 1988, McKean removed himself as lead evangelist of the Boston church and appointed himself as Missions Evangelist, assuming a role similar to that of the Apostle Paul.[18] He appointed nine men as his "Focused

Few,"[19] later called World Sector Leaders. The focus of the movement was to plant new churches throughout the world. The Boston movement's mission is to evangelize the world within one generation.

McKean eventually settled in Los Angeles, and lives there when he's not traveling in his role of World Missions Evangelist. Meanwhile, the Boston church began floundering in terms of growth. In May 1990 Al Baird was removed from his position as permanent lead evangelist of that church, and McKean's brother, Randy, was appointed to the position.[20] With McKean in Los Angeles, the church there became the "Super Church" and remains the focus of leadership training. At this point, when churches were reconstructed, the leaders of those churches were more often brought to Los Angeles for "retraining." Once called "the Jerusalem of the modern-day movement," Boston was no longer the seat of the movement. At the 1993 World Leadership Conference in Los Angeles, a new name for the movement was announced: the International Churches of Christ.

On February 4, 1994, McKean and his World Sector Leaders signed the Evangelization Proclamation.[21] At that time, the movement had "planted" 146 churches in 53 nations and claimed an attendance of 75,000. It is important to bear in mind that the International Churches of Christ movement is not to be confused with the mainline Churches of Christ, from which it grew, or with the United Church of Christ with which it has never had a connection.

Notes

1. Terris, D. "Come, All Ye Faithful," *Boston Globe,* June 8, 1986.
2. Statement of the Congregation, Crossroads Church of Christ, Aug. 21, 1985.

3. Boston Church of Christ bulletin, Apr. 22, 1984.
4. McKean, K. "Revolution Through Restoration," *Upside Down*, Issue Two, 1992.
5. Terris.
6. Andorfer, B. "Crossroads: Its Dramatic Growth Is Accompanied by Reputation of Aggressiveness, Mind Control," *Gainesville Sun*, Feb. 17, 1979.
7. Pugh, J. "Crossroads: Fundamentalist church gathers campus converts ... and critics," *St. Petersburg Times*, Jul. 21, 1979.
8. Pugh.
9. Noles, R. "Crossroads: Parents, Pastor say it's a dangerous cult," *St Petersburg Times*, Apr. 12, 1979.
10. Pugh.
11. Noles, R. "St. Pete parents band together to fight Crossroads," *St. Petersburg Times*, Aug. 16, 1979.
12. Noles, "Crossroads: Parents, Pastor say."
13. Noles, "St. Pete parents band together,"
14. Noles, "Crossroads: Parents, Pastor say," "St. Pete parents band together"; Pugh.
15. Pugh.
16. Noles, "St. Pete parents band together."
17. Audiotape of congregational meeting, Crossroads Church of Christ (2 tapes), June 26, 1988.
18. Wooten, M. "Kip McKean Enters Full-Time Mission Work," *Discipleship Magazine*, Summer 1988.
19. Boston Church of Christ bulletin, Sept. 4, 1988.
20. Audiotape of congregational meeting, Boston Church of Christ, May 6, 1990.
21. Boston Church of Christ bulletin, "The Evangelization Proclamation," Feb. 13, 1994.

2

The Boston Church of Christ
at Boston University

Robert Watts Thornburg

Seven years ago under tremendous pressure of distraught parents, anxious college administrators, concerned chaplains, and friends who had lost friends, I dashed off this article telling what I had seen and known of the Boston Church of Christ at Boston University: how it worked, and what one might do when confronted by the wreckage it produced. My office has distributed more than twenty thousand copies to individuals attending meetings and others who called in to ask if we knew anything about this group which strikes such fear into those who are confronted with it. Countless others have requested and received permission to reprint and distribute it. How I wish I had kept track of everywhere it has gone!

Now after the invitation of those who are preparing this volume, I had first thought it would be better to write an historical piece describing the first days and the development of this organization. Instead, I am submitting this addendum to the original instead of beginning anew—for this original article, now more than seven years old, bears a most eloquent testimony to some of the salient facts of the Multiplying Ministries.

Critical Perspectives

It is fair to say that what is now called the International Churches of Christ (ICC) had its beginnings in that little Lexington, Massachusetts, church in the fall of 1979, after one false start at Eastern Illinois State College. While there is some residue from Crossroads Ministry in which Kip McKean was originally trained and started his ministry, I suspect that we can believe the testimony of the leadership of the ICC that its development is unique and separate from anything that went before.

It should be noted that some of the basic written texts used in the Boston Church of Christ, and recommended for further study in the process of discipling, are classics in the field of church growth; but when it comes to the actual way in which the organization operated in Boston or Hong Kong or Dallas or Madrid, the methods as well as the dynamic bear the distinctive and personal touch of Kip himself. There is no other source for information, inspiration, or interpretation than the one who stands at the peak of this truly "awesome" monolithic pyramid.

What Remains the Same

While the history of the movement must be updated, and some current organizational dynamic discussed, the guts of the method remain unchanged since 1988 when this piece was originally written. When I look at the changes in the rest of our nation, culture, and society, it seems truly remarkable that the ICC's methods of recruitment and indoctrination still use the same words and illustrations that were current when the movement was just ten years old and had members in lots fewer places, both in the United States and around the world. More than vivid fulfillment of the adage "If it ain't broke, don't fix it," the constancy of the basic methodology is consistent with the major reason for their so-called success. It is the fact of constancy and total security in a world of such tremendous flux and change which seems to draw persons to the organization. There is no cry for relevance—for, after all, they are telling folks that this was just the way Jesus did it, and their version of that develops only incrementally over the years as pragmatic needs dictate.

This document was originally written to be distributed on the campus of Boston University. It was aimed at students, dormitory Resident Assistants, roommates, parents, and friends. Over time, more and more people came into our offices asking, "Do you know anything about the church group that meets in the Boston Garden? I think my friend may be involved in it. I am worried about what it's doing to him. What can I do about it?" In response I felt it was necessary to put out, as we described it in the school brochure, "information that may be vital to your religious and emotional health."

A Brief History

The Boston Church of Christ began in 1979 when evangelist Kip McKean, who had been dismissed from a local church near Eastern Illinois State College, came to Massachusetts to take over the Lexington Church of Christ. At the time, that parish was a very small unit of the large and established group called the Churches of Christ.

The Churches of Christ is an American denomination that traces its roots back to the early eighteenth century to a preacher named Alexander Campbell. Campbell hoped to organize a group of churches that patterned its worship and life after the church of the New Testament. He called his dream the Restoration Movement, and during the past 150 years, the Churches of Christ grew into 18,000 parishes with 2.5 million members.

The Churches of Christ are very prominent in the southeastern and south central regions of the United States. They make very large use of nonordained (lay) leadership, and use no instruments in their worship except the human voice. Conservative in their theology, they have little or no cooperation or association with other religious organizations. They are, however, respected as a strong and stable highly independent religious movement.

While McKean and the followers he brought with him had the name and many of the marks of the Restoration Movement, they had added very special methods to the recruitment and indoctrination of new members into their church. McKean, along with some other college students, had been introduced to this evangelical method through a campus ministry in Gainesville, Florida, which had begun in the Crossroads Church of Christ. They had developed a plan for church recruitment that took the name of the church and was called the Crossroads Method of discipling. It is often referred to as a multiplying ministry. Their discipling involved highly structured personal instruction within a tight hierarchical system of authority. It was so intense that it gained early success on many college campuses all over the country after 1971.

The Unique Aspects of the Boston Church of Christ
The Lexington Church of Christ soon had to move from its first building, and in quick succession members found themselves in Arlington, then in the Boston Opera House (where they changed their name to the Boston Church of Christ), and finally in the Boston Garden. From 1980 until

THE BOSTON MOVEMENT

May of 1988 the church printed in their weekly newspaper the names of each newly baptized person. Church attendance and baptisms grew rapidly. Financial support likewise continued to grow at rather remarkable rates.

When church historians look back on the religious history of the United States in the last quarter of the twentieth century, I believe that the organization and the growth of the Boston Church of Christ will be considered a very special phenomenon. Anyone who believes that growth in numbers and in financial support is the single criterion for success in a religious organization would certainly have to say that the Boston Church of Christ is very successful.

On the other hand, there has scarcely been a time in U.S. religious history when the name of a religious organization has struck such fear and apprehension into the hearts of so many people as does the name of the Boston Church of Christ on this campus, and around the country. Not uncommon were calls to me from academic colleagues—such as a dean of students at Arizona State University, a professor at the University of Michigan, and a chaplain at Columbia University in New York—asking how their campuses might deal with the tactics of the Boston Church "plantings" in their communities. Clearly this is not simply a local phenomenon.

A television reporter once asked me quite naturally whether my concerns about the Boston movement, as it's sometimes called, were shared by others at the university and around the city of Boston. I suggested that he go alone into the Student Union where many students are congregating and ask the first ten students he met whether they knew about the Boston Church of Christ. He returned to report that eight of the first ten had been approached by members of the group in ways that they found intrusive and offensive. On a recent Boston radio talk show, when a caller mentioned the group, the program producer reported that the station's phone lines were clogged by those who wanted to confirm the same high-pressure recruitment techniques. Chaplains and college and university student affairs personnel from the entire area have experienced the same complaints from students in their schools.

Boston University and the Boston Church of Christ
Boston University was organized originally as a small Methodist center for ministerial training in 1849, the same year in which Alexander Campbell began the Restoration Movement. By 1869 the small school had moved twice to finally locate in Boston, where three wealthy businessmen interested in quality higher education in a Christian context were crucial in organizing the new Boston University. These men were such strict and committed Methodists that it never occurred to them to mention any legal or organizational tie of the new school with the denomination they loved. But they were distinctive in one historically significant way. From its inception, Boston University was guided by a Charter principle that stated unequivocally that no student or faculty should be denied admission to the new school on account of gender, race, or religious beliefs.

That principle has been most important in the school's development. Boston University was the nation's first institution of higher education to admit women to all of its professional programs; thus, the university has a long distinguished list of female alumni who are leaders in every profession. Equally notable was the fact that persons of color were to be admitted to all of the university's programs. Martin

Luther King, Jr.—one of our most distinguished alumni—was but one in a long line of important black leaders who received degrees from Boston University's graduate school and professional colleges. However, the parallel declaration of religious toleration has been increasingly taken for granted as the United States as a whole grew progressively less sectarian.

As U.S. society has grown more secular, we have retained a "respect" for religious activities and interests. Every Gallup Poll shows that a high percentage of Americans say they trust clergy and the church in spite of the recent scandals; an even higher percentage say they believe in God. But this respect does not include the same critical elements of examination and analysis that we apply to our political, economic, or scientific enterprises. As a result, our society has been exposed to all manner of abuses and indignities in the name of religion. As a society, we do not seem to have the ability to make the critical distinctions in religious practice between the helpful and the genuinely destructive.

In a society in which religion has often been a divisive rather than a unifying factor, I have a vision that this campus could be a paradigm of genuine religious understanding. Pluralism at its best is not persons who are ignorant of and unimpressed with the religious beliefs and practices of others, but those who are able to learn and enrich their own faith and practices by their new and growing understanding of other historic faith systems. I believe that this is not only a worthy goal, but one which has begun to see significant fulfillment. In my own observation of the campus, a major obstacle to healthy religious growth and mutual understanding is found in the methods and abuses of the Boston Church of Christ.

Throughout Boston University's long history of theological openness, and our current situation of religious

14

tolerance and understanding, the university's actions with respect to the Boston Church of Christ are all the more remarkable. For what must be the first time in the university's history, leaders of a religious group have been formally and officially banned or, more exactly, sanctioned from coming onto the campus.

Why was such an action deemed necessary? What does it mean on the campus today, and what should those who are concerned about the activities of this group do?

Can a Religious Group Really Be Destructive?
In order to answer the question, Can a religious group really be destructive?, we must establish some definitions and distinctions. It is vital to separate beliefs from behaviors. This is important for two reasons.

First and most important is the fact that a university campus is the very last place in the world where there should be any suppression of ideas or beliefs. At best we are in the business of seeking to understand, analyze, and critique theories and notions in science and technology, in political and ethical thought, and in spiritual and theological opinions. In no manner does the process of analysis include the suppression of ideas, even though we may believe them to be ill conceived.

The second factor is the recognition that we can and must be concerned about behavior that hurts students or tends to undermine the essential purposes for which the university exists. When such behaviors can be clearly identified, and warnings can be issued concerning the repeated practice of such destructive behaviors, then the university can legally and legitimately take decisive actions to protect our students and other members of the community from such behaviors.

A major conflict arises at this point. Some of the behaviors that are most injurious to our students are born from and nurtured within the essential beliefs of the Boston Church. In most cases, then, we must identify and understand the belief or doctrine that informs those behaviors that are considered to be destructive. In no case have we infringed on the right of individual students to hold and practice their religious beliefs, even beliefs that we may find highly dangerous. Both the First Amendment to the United States Constitution and Boston University's own Charter specifically forbid that. But when a person's practice of religious faith adversely affects others in the community, then it is not only reasonable but necessary that decisive and appropriate actions be taken.

We must carefully and specifically define the destructive activities and behaviors. When these definitions have been made clear to students and staff, then the university has both the right and the obligation to protect students from false and deceptive activities that harm students and threaten the full and healthy development of learning and faith on the campus.

What Is Destructive About
the Boston Church of Christ?

I summarize here literally hundreds of reports from members and ex-members of the group. In many cases the concerns expressed in these reports were presented personally by me to the various campus ministers assigned to Boston University by the Boston Church, as well as to Dr. Albert Baird, the elder of the church at that time. Usually they accepted our complaints, suggesting that they had never really understood our concerns or regulations. Often they told me that my concerns were completely justified but were probably caused entirely by the excessive zeal of new converts. Initially, I accepted those explanations, especially when they were accompanied with the pledge that things would improve. They did not.

Thus, at the September 1987 meeting of the Religious Life Council of Boston University, it was concluded by those present that the leadership of the Boston Church, despite their claims of innocence, were either unwilling or unable to change their procedures. Our concerns can be grouped under several major categories of destructive activities.

1. Recruitment techniques include the duplicitous use of love and high-pressure harassment, producing incredibly high levels of induced guilt.
Loneliness and isolation are the standard marks of a large urban college campus. Students in their first experience of college often feel a tremendous need for friendship and companionship. Perhaps the most wonderful human aspect of college life is the friendships made during that time, which often continue through associations throughout the rest of life. When love is contrived or false or used only for the sake of gaining another goal—namely, more members for the group—that certainly is a duplicitous use of love.

All the literature on destructive cults includes the concept of "love bombing," an approach used with great skill by recruiters from the Boston Church. Find someone vulnerable—this is their first rule of recruitment. Some members still cherish the notion that they are working to save a soul, but the real concern is to get a new member into the

17

organization. If someone is eating alone, walking alone, clearly disturbed by some bad news, or just terribly anxious to make some friends on campus, then that person is genuinely vulnerable to an approach using false love.

The first days of college life are so exciting. But students are also vulnerable. Knowing this, recruiters make themselves immediately available to help a new student carry trunks or to provide directions or engage in a "friendly" opening conversation. Under almost any other circumstances that would be excellent. But when every move is made for the single purpose of urging a person to go to a Bible Talk or some other church meeting, that type of behavior constitutes a false use of the most basic aspect of Christian faith—love.

Once a contact is made, and addresses or phone numbers exchanged, the pressure begins. Phone calls are often and urgent. There is no rest from them. The phone rings late at night to urge the new contact to attend a meeting tomorrow, or a note is under the door, or suddenly there is a "random" meeting on campus. Although at first this might seem a bit intense, it is also rather flattering to think that these people care enough to expend all that energy. If it were genuine, it would be a transforming power; but, in fact, it is done only for the purpose of getting a new person to a Bible Talk in order to work toward an association with a prayer partner, or discipler.

Then the guilt induction begins in earnest: "If I have done all this for you, certainly you will be willing to go with me to my meeting, and meet my friends." During the first meetings with these "instant best friends," they ask more questions: Where are you from? What is your major? What other interests do you have? What are the things that are most important to you? With what seems like incredible coincidence, the recruiter is always interested in exactly the same things as the new prospect.

After a few meetings, church recruiters will begin to ask about more personal matters, such as "Where do you need prayer the most?" The purpose here is to find where they can expose and manipulate a person's feelings of inadequacy and fear. The use of guilt as a basic motive for recruitment and training is extremely basic to the Boston Church. Long after individuals are out of the group, they are left with a sense of fear and guilt. It is strong and powerful and very destructive.

2. The training process is a virtual cloning of one person by his or her prayer partner in a totally authoritarian relationship with no rights of personal choice or interpretation.
Recruiters say they want to engage in study of the Bible. In truth, the new prospect is entering the most tightly controlled, coordinated program of thought reform and manipulation. Its single purpose is to establish in the recruit's mind the message that all hope of salvation belongs only to this one ten-year-old local church. Using a very limited number of single-verse Bible texts, the person leading the study draws the prospect into a simplistically tight theological pattern.

Leaders and members repeat over and over that they are only following what the Bible says. In fact, they are using minute portions of scripture, all of which are taught through interpretations that twist and contort the simple meaning of the words in order to match the group's doctrinal teachings. There is wide use of memorization of single-sentence texts, always accompanied with a strict interpretation of the group's understanding of the meaning of those texts.

THE BOSTON MOVEMENT

At first, those who ask questions are put off: "That's a very good question," the leaders say, "but if you'll hold it for just a minute we'll come back to it." Problem is, they never deal with anything outside their tightly controlled belief system. In matters of interpretation, total authority is vested in the leaders. Any right of personal interpretation is expressly and explicitly forbidden, and interpretation is not based on a consensus of members, scholars, or any others than the leaders of this one movement.

Outsiders who have spoken to members of the Boston movement have had the same experience. Having been given a copy of an early training manual, *First Principles*, I knew that their use of scripture did not include the so-called parable of the Final Judgment in the last part of the 25th chapter of the Gospel of Matthew. I confronted one of their students who affirmed that I did not know or believe the Bible. When I said that was totally false, I asked what he made of the passage, in which Jesus clearly and specifically says who gets into Heaven and who goes to Hell and why. The student obviously had never heard the passage; but when I told the story and asked what he made of it, he replied without hesitation: "They haven't told us yet."

The training is simplistic, completely authoritarian, and absolutely identical from one person to the next. Such a structure makes for much greater efficiency in the training process, and for total orthodoxy among all members. The discipling process can be studied with rather great ease since it is a virtual cloning process: every person is molded into the same intellectual and personality fit.

Flavil Yeakley, Jr., head of the Church Growth Institute for the Churches of Christ, was invited some years ago by the local leadership of the Boston movement to study

20

nine hundred of its members. Using the Myers-Briggs Personality Inventory, Yeakley concluded that serious emotional damage was being done to members of the Boston Church of Christ by coercing them into a single personality type in order to ensure conformity. This is done, according to the leaders who responded to the study, to remold all converts into the image of Jesus. In Myers-Briggs terminology, Jesus was an ESFJ (extroverted, sensing, feeling, judging) personality type, and every member must be the same. In my personal judgment, such a claim strikes somewhere between arrogant stupidity and blasphemous distortion. Yeakley's book, *The Discipling Dilemma*, is an excellent resource for further study of the group.

Not only are the methods used to indoctrinate members destructive to human growth and personal freedom, but these methods clearly cut directly across most of the purposes and methods for which any institution of higher learning stands.

3. Using methods that represent classic examples of thought-reform techniques, the Boston Church of Christ discourages new prospects from associating with nonmembers, systematically cutting out any contact with family, friends, or outside sources of reality checks.

Besides the indoctrination just described, new prospects in the Boston Church are systematically cut away from all contact with anyone not associated with the church. This is usually the first place where a person's participation can be recognized by a friend, a parent, or a roommate. A student will begin to receive an inordinately large number of phone calls from these "new friends," and suddenly has no time to talk to or associate with those who are not involved. It is often noted that members of the church will accompany newer members from class to class, meet them after school, and spend all possible free time in conversation and activities with them.

Parents and any former friends are also regarded by the group as very suspect. Generally, it is suggested to new converts that their new faith probably will not be understood or accepted by their parents. Although leaders regularly deny such claims, it has been my repeated experience that new members are told that their parents are not Christian, no matter what their professed religion or involvement in church activities, and that since parents are "of the devil," they would best be avoided. Hundreds of parents have called me in literal anguish over the responses they have received from their children. The Boston Church's justification for this action is a strangely brittle interpretation of Luke 14:26, which they read to imply that if a person does not hate mother and father, then that person cannot belong to Christ. Any reasonable study of Christian scripture and Christian practice certainly will not support that claim.

In like manner, persons in other Christian organizations are not considered Christians. In response to a direct and specific question, a Boston Church campus ministry leader told a group of students whom I was addressing that no Catholics could be Christian or could enter the Kingdom of God because Catholics followed "traditions of men" rather than the Bible. Student members have told me that Mother Teresa could not be a Christian for the same reason. Such a stand is often softened or skirted in public discussion since it sounds harsh even by their own standards.

If all Catholics are going to Hell, other Christian groups do no better in the eyes of the Boston Church. All the mainline churches are doomed, as are other Churches of Christ, which Boston Church leaders describe as dead and spiritless. And we who lead such groups are of the devil because we lead others away from the "truth." In response to this claim, I continue to assert the strong Biblical affirmation that all matters of final judgment and eternal destiny for each of us are still the prerogative of the Eternal God, and neither any church nor any leader has been designated to make that decision about any other person's life.

4. Once established as the sole dispenser of salvation, the group dominates every moment of the day, demanding attendance at every meeting of the organization.
The Boston Church becomes counterproductive, if not destructive, to any important discipline of study. Church leaders require attendance at every one of the meetings even though they may conflict with academic requirements or family obligations. When someone says, "I have to study for a test," the typical reply is, "Which is more important to you, mere grades or Jesus?" This becomes an effective and powerful guilt trip.

Members are required to go to Bible Talks each week, plus the house church meeting, a social evening, the Sunday service, as well as spend time with their discipler in continued Bible study and training. Few students can excel in schoolwork under these conditions, although there have been some exceptions who are regularly used by the Boston Church as examples. By far, a much larger number of students show either a precipitous grade drop or leave school entirely.

For leaders of the Boston Movement, that outcome is not that tragic because they affirm that full-time evangelistic work is the only really authentic Christian vocation for a man. There are two parts to examine in that statement.

First, one can see their exclusive emphasis on evangelistic ministry as the only valid and ultimately significant form of work for a Christian. For example, the local Boston Church was known to celebrate the departure of two black physicians from the practice of medicine in their community in order to become leaders in new plantings of the Boston Church. Most Christian churches hold that all vocations can be a form of ministry if done in obedience to the will of God. Such emphasis on preaching and pastoral ministry as the only ultimately acceptable form of work causes many students to either drop out of professional programs or change their major. Leadership in the church or any of its smaller units does not require any extensive scholarship, but only more intense discipling—that is, further indoctrination into the church's very closed system of beliefs and behavior.

Second, the statement highlights the role of women in the Boston Church. Women have no place in the overall church leadership. They are allowed to disciple other women, but are urged to be supportive and submissive to their husbands. They may never expect to rise above second-class status within the church. Further, members are told often that they must date and marry, as well as often being told whom to date. As in other aspects of the church, everyone is expected to conform to a single style of life: to be married, and then to propagate. Being single, while not explicitly condemned, is never encouraged.

Along with the total domination of time comes a significant requirement to give money to the church. While they refer to the Bible notion of the tithe (10 percent of total income), the actual requirements are much greater. I have in my possession a computer-generated invoice for $20.00 per Sunday sent to a student who goes to Boston University on a full-tuition scholarship-for-need. I am not sure what income figure was used to determine that his tithe should be $20.00, but this far exceeds any Biblical standards I know.

The same guilt that enforces attendance at meetings serves to motivate such giving. And again, this tactic is very successful from the standpoint of the development of the organization. The church newspaper dated May 21, 1987, reported that the church received $94,953 on a budget newly raised to $100,000 a week. That goal will produce over five million dollars a year. So far, former members are the only ones to have raised questions as to where that much money goes.

The church also reports an offering for the "poor." It has remained at about $3,000 a week for the past eighteen months [at the time of writing this paper], while the budget for the church work continues to rise. The Boston Church of Christ is also known to say that the poor are always those within the church organization who are having difficulty. Thus, nonmembers can expect nothing from them.

5. When total submission is acknowledged in a re-baptism, then the standard of faithfulness is measured by the number of recruits each member can bring into the organization.
Formal acceptance into the Boston Church takes place with baptism. This is nearly always a re-baptism, since the church considers no other baptism as valid, even a baptism within other Churches of Christ. Baptism is also the moment of salvation. Often active members are re-baptized yet again when they are known to have been less than perfect in their

faith and practice. At times, baptism is rushed upon the new members after two or three weeks of association with the church. This is particularly true for a person who the recruiter believes might be swayed by friends, family, or other outside influences to not affiliate with the church.

Once baptized, the member is responsible to bring others into the group. While there is some dispute on this point, it has been reported by many ex-members that they were given a quota of persons to evangelize; this was meant to show loyalty and devotion to the practice of their faith. The pressure of the recruitment process described earlier is much more understandable in the context of realizing that the quality of a member's faith, and ultimately one's eternal salvation, depends entirely on the "fruits" of the faith—fruits being exclusively defined as bringing new persons into the organization.

Against that kind of motivation and that level of guilt production, the mere rules of the university or other limitations put on the church seem inconsequential. It becomes rather apparent that the leadership has neither the intention nor the power to limit instances of overzealous solicitation given the guidance that informs it.

Do we have any right to judge these activities as destructive? Yes, indeed! While we continue to stand firmly for the rights of individuals to practice faith each in their own way, we also have responsibilities to protect students from harassment, coercion, and manipulation—whether conscious or unconscious—and protect them from the intense peer pressure the Boston Church exerts on its members. It is not that individuals are tricked per se into joining the church, but once someone has entered the church's sphere of influence, the peer pressure and guilt induction are fierce and practically impossible to resist. For most college students, peer pressure is the strongest force in their lives.

I believe that some few persons have been helped by the Boston Church of Christ's highly structured and authoritarian approach to religious practice. Nevertheless, the environment within the Boston movement is a kind of spiritual prison in which personal and intellectual conformity is demanded and coerced by the power of peer pressure. When that peer pressure is combined with the doctrine that this church alone is the Kingdom of God, and that outside the church there is no salvation, then members lose all freedom of faith and conscience, and that is indeed destructive. In my judgment, it is more destructive than any possible benefits.

What Can a Friend or Parent Do to Help Someone Who Is Already Involved?

1. Don't condemn another's involvement in the Boston Church; but don't give up on them as a friend. Members have been told that if they are faithful to the church's practices, they will be condemned by those outside the church. If you do exactly that, you will fulfill that expectation, further convincing the members they are being good members no matter what arguments are posed to them. On the positive side, keep up all contacts. While members will probably turn down your invitations to meals or other activities, keep making the offer and let them know that you really care about them.

2. Don't try to argue Biblical or theological points, but encourage members to talk about how they feel and believe. In *Combating Cult Mind Control*, Steve Hassan writes, "A common mistake is that relatives try to argue the person out

of involvement by using a condescending, confrontational approach. Rational discussions are simply not effective with someone who has been indoctrinated with mind control." Be positive. Ask the members to talk in their own words, describe their own experiences rather than use the words they have been taught. Do your best to engage them in a thoughtful discussion without being confrontational. Often, when members hear themselves say aloud to a Catholic roommate that all Catholics are going to Hell because they're not members of the Boston Church of Christ, this will help jolt them into a new reality—an outcome that your arguments or pleading are not likely to produce.

3. Help members to recall activities and associations they had before they were in the group. Look at pictures of fun times and places, bring in old friends, help them remember what they were like and interested in before they got involved with the Boston Church.

4. Work to build up the sense of self-worth and personal pride which has been broken down by association with the group. The thought-reform processes used to bring people into the Boston Church revolve around reducing members' feelings of personal worth and sense of pride. This is primarily done by constantly requiring members to share all of their deepest secrets of the past on the theory that the discipling partner can somehow remove those so-called stains of guilt.

Actually, the effect of this constant replaying of past weaknesses is not to bring about healthy spiritual growth and personal development; rather, it serves to fully collapse the individual's ego strength so that the person becomes prepared to take on the image and personality of the Boston Church member without any sense of personal identity or individual freedom. Being reduced to "nothing," the person can then be rebuilt in the image desired by the group.

The standard that Jesus gives in his own summary of the Law says in part that *you shall love your neighbor as you love yourself.* The self-hatred that is standard fare in the guilt training of the Bible Talks must be countered by positive healthy love. You should show members that they have talent and personality and love to give, which have been knocked out of them in their current association. God loves you for what you are, not for your membership or activities in the Boston Church.

5. Keep your own faith alive, and let the other person know that you are also concerned about spiritual and moral values. College is a time for testing the traditional values of your family and your childhood religion. It's quite common for students to take a vacation from God for the first years of their college experience. Many who are rethinking their traditional religious faith are the prospects who will most easily be recruited by the Boston Church. At Boston University, the number of former Roman Catholics who have been drawn into the Boston Church is staggering.

If you are a Catholic, invite your friends who are curious about the Boston Church to go with you to Mass. If you are a Protestant, invite those who are being courted by the Boston Church to go with you to the chapel or Protestant groups. The most effective way to deal with destructive religious practices is to give good evidence of what a strong and inquiring faith would look like.

While I would like to encourage vital religious faith in every student, I do not want to imply that a person should practice faith only as a means to get someone else out of a destructive religious practice. One thing seems very clear: authentic religious practice in Christianity or Judaism or any religion should produce people who are stronger and better integrated in their faith with decent values, a good moral code, and vocational and relational goals. When you demonstrate something better than what they see in the Boston Church, you won't need to make arguments to persuade them.

6. Boston University has provided strong support to help students help others to avoid unwanted harassment and solicitation by any group. Several years ago the Dean of Students sent a letter to every student in the Residence Halls clearly stating that students are free to join and actively participate in any religious group of their choice. But students also have the right to say a clear and unmistakable no to any unwanted solicitation or harassment to join a group.

The Dean's letter further stated that the failure of any student to respect that clear no can result in disciplinary action. The letter included a list of the university chaplains who are ready to help Resident Assistants or concerned roommates or parents in dealing with the organizations that are destructive to a student's life, work, and faith. It is important that incidents of flagrant violation of this requirement be reported.

Because most students need and want to be liked, they are sometimes hesitant to bring any charge against a fellow student, no matter how difficult or painful the harassment. Remember, there is no more stigma to reporting religious harassment than there is to reporting sexual or racial harassment.

7. Boston University has set up support groups for former members of destructive groups—religious or otherwise. The support group can help participants sort out their feelings and get back into the mainstream of life. A group called FOCUS meets every month at the chapel; it is led entirely by ex-members of various destructive groups.

It has been our sad experience that few clergy will be trusted by those who have been badly scarred by the authoritarian leadership of the Boston Church. Likewise, because they are not yet sufficiently aware of the methods of a group such as the Boston Church, most therapists are not immediately effective.

There is a significant and growing number of former members who work as exit counselors and cult education specialists for those who wish to regain a healthy, vital religious and personal life. These persons are not the deprogrammers so often featured in the media. They are not involved with kidnapping, physical force, or intense emotional coercion. They work with family members and friends to bring a person back into solid and healthy relationships with parents, siblings, spouses, and former friends. Here again, it is wise to contact one of the chaplains to get the names and phone numbers of such persons.

How Can You Keep from Getting Involved in a Destructive Religious Group?

1. Learn to be a questioner! Ask very specific questions when you are invited to a religious organization. What is the name? With whom are they affiliated? How do they relate to your own faith tradition or to any other religious organizations?

When any church or religious group claims to have all the truth to the exclusion of any other group, it is time to be very suspicious of that group. The wonders of the love of God in our creation and daily life are much too powerful and exhaustive to be contained in one set of doctrines or beliefs.

If you find questions are evaded or put off, it is likely that the group has something to hide, something they do not want you to know about them. With any clergy or professor on campus, an honest question deserves a straightforward and honest answer. When you do not receive that kind of response, there is danger.

2. Start forming a strong and lasting community with your friends. Destructive groups nearly always approach persons who are alone. For those of us who enjoy being alone, that can be a problem, so be on the alert.

In general, the college experience is a time when you will make many friends who will stay with you throughout your life. Such friendship is not that of the "instant" friend produced by love-bombing techniques, so-called friends who will be with you only so long as you are a prospect for membership or active in the life of their organization. Genuine friends go with you through all the phases and changes of college life, and do not predicate friendship on your willingness to be exactly as they are or to believe exactly as they do.

I know many people who are never approached by overly eager solicitors for quick-fix religions. Those are persons who have support groups of other students who care about them and associate with them even when they are sad or out of sorts. That is a healthy relationship, not one that demands a plastic smile and a phony confidence in every situation.

3. Be able to say no, which is not as easy as it may sound. College students want to be accepted; they usually do not wish to be rude. Also, many students are shy, and will do anything to avoid closing the doors on someone else or doing something that would otherwise alienate someone. First-year students in particular, because of peer pressure, typically do lots of things they would never have dreamed of doing before, thinking, "Oh, everybody's doing it." Certainly that applies to use of drugs and alcohol, to sexual involvements, and even to some dishonesty in exams. When you are lonesome and see two or three very friendly students who tell you how great you are, usually you don't stop to ask, "Are they for real? Are these people interested in me, or just looking for another member of their group?"

The best measure I know for growing maturity is to develop standards and ideals that give you the basis for saying a clear and resounding no when someone suggests you do something you know to be unwise. Real friends will accept the standards you set, rather than try to coerce you into their standards or group.

Conclusion

Religious faith should be a vital and informative part of the growing years of college. But a faith that will be adequate to inform all of life's decisions and strengthen you through all the years to come requires study, personal experiences, and testing. I believe that such a faith should be enriched by understanding traditions that are very different from the faith into which you were born. Such enrichment is never a threat to true faith. Always be suspicious of those who tell you that they have the only truth or the only way on any subject. They are either arrogant and uninformed, or destructive.

THE BOSTON MOVEMENT

Ours is a society in which strong religious and family standards appear to be under attack from so many different quarters. It is in the midst of such uncertainty that we are tempted to respond to anyone or any group that pretends to have all the truth and *the* answer to every intellectual, theological, and moral problem. Strong religious faith is one that has grown along with all the other aspects of our life—social, political, vocational, moral, and relational. Strong faith should be an informative and integrating part of all of our experiences.

Faith occasionally is destructive and divisive. Certainly it is in the case of the Boston Church of Christ. But encountering that destructiveness ought to help move us to something more constructive, not force us to shy away from the strength and support of constructive faith.

This is the end of the original 1988 article.

What Has Changed Since 1988?

As I have suggested, the remarkable thing about the history of the Boston Church of Christ (now International Churches of Christ) is that their central strategies and activities have remained virtually untouched since the high point of their existence in Boston in 1988. There are, however, several important new factors that affect their destructive activities on campus and in the community. These factors also should have an impact on the ways in which campus student personnel and chaplains respond in order to be helpful to students.

1. Central headquarters move, and continued expansion.
We may never know the full truth concerning the reasons for moving the headquarters of the newly named International

Churches of Christ (ICC) to Los Angeles, but the results have been twofold. Any sense of creative change for the movement here has gone out, and the organization has entered what would be called (in other phases of church history) a scholastic phase. This is characterized by greater intensity and commitment to the basic principles of organization and development.

Randy McKean, Kip's brother, has been the leader of the Boston Church, but unlike his older brother, Randy has virtually no visibility in the community. He simply does not have the charismatic personality of the founder.

It has been reported by many persons who have exited the church that the move was made because the expansion in Boston had leveled off, and the core leadership wished to be in a place where there was greater opportunity for the phenomenal growth that had characterized Boston in the first few years.

With the removal of much of the more dynamic church leadership away from the Boston area, the overall level of vitality has ebbed away, and the number of persons dropping out of the movement has soared. Many college campuses have groups of ex-members of the Boston Church. Some form as support groups or join in assisting others who have fled the church; whenever one needs to have an ex-member available to assist someone out of the group, one seems to be available.

I can nearly map the expanding area of plantings of the ICC by the telephone calls I receive from campus newspapers or student personnel leaders. Smaller Midwestern towns that have significant student populations are now asking: "What can we do? They are disrupting our campus." On some campuses the ICC groups use the name "The Upside-down

Club," which refers to the response to the first Christians in the book of Acts. But the nature of the disruptions which the ICC brings is much different from the blessings of the Spirit which the first disciples gave to those whom they met. It has remained curious to me that questions of concern come from Deans of Students or Directors of Campus Activities many more times than from chaplains or other campus ministers.

2. Increased publicity requires some new twists in recruitment.

When my 1988 paper was published, it was in very high demand because very little had been written about the activities and aims of the Boston movement. By now campus newspapers in nearly every major urban center have carried one or more stories concerning the chaos caused by the group. Usually the depth and insights of these campus newspaper stories are much better than those that have appeared in many metropolitan daily papers. They are replete with quotations from students who have left the group or roommates who have lost friends to it.

Articles in metropolitan newspapers, as well as coverage by national media, have usually been brief, timid, and often inaccurate. In many cases, reporters have found serious and flagrant abuses, and prepared drafts that report exactly what they have seen, only to be told by editors and legal departments that such stories about religious organizations should be cut down in length and toned down in passion. Legal actions brought by the Church of Scientology and the Way International have cast a very uneasy blanket over newspapers that are clear and forthright in dealing with stories in other areas of the society.

Critical Perspectives

Television, both local and national, has had very uneven results. My own first meeting with Al Baird, now the official TV spokesperson of the group, occurred about 1984 after a local Boston TV news magazine carried an interview in which I said some rather critical things about the methods of the movement. My words were probably magnified some by the fact that the other half of the program was devoted to the activities of the Church of Scientology. Dr. Baird's first response to me was that he did not want his group to be mentioned in the same program with those "Cults."

There have been at least two national programs that have devoted segments to the Boston movement: *20/20* did a piece in which John Stossell did the interviews. It sought to give equal time to those who were for and against. As a result, it had a pale pablum effect. I had several conversations with the producer of the program, on the day of the airing. It was very clear from his questions that ABC's legal department was playing a very careful card. When I have shown the clip of the program to students, the high point of the screening has been the students' response to the closing remarks by Hugh Downs. After shaking his head at these "charges" which had been reported, he soberly announced that he was surprised that students would be so naive as to get involved in such a group. All the students with whom I have watched this program laugh in disbelief at his naïveté.

The much more sensational *Inside Edition* did a much more informative and provocative story. The high point was a hidden camera and microphone (both legal in the State of New York), which the producer took into his conversations with his discipler. He had gone to the New York Church of Christ as an inquirer and clearly recorded the words and the pressure brought to bear on persons who come close into the

37

process. The main inquiry made by the discipler was about the sexual activities of the subject with particular regard to homosexuality, incest, and bestiality, to which the producer pleaded innocent on all scores. The "out-takes" of these conversations were much more devastating than those that were actually aired, but they often required interpretation or understanding of the methods being used to make sense.

Later the reporter asked Dr. Baird about the so-called "sin-list" which the leaders of the group compiled on each member. Baird defended the practice, but often I have heard ex-members say that such information was used as a none-too-subtle pressure to keep people in the organization if they had thoughts of leaving.

On campus, the most important educational and informational activities about the dangers of destructive religious activities in general, and the Boston Church in particular, are found in training or orientation sessions for new students and student leaders. Some campus leaders make the assumption that after only one program, all necessary information is disseminated. But since one fourth of the student body changes each year, annual repeats are done, which helps to effectively control the group. On our campus, leaders of many para-church evangelical groups who feel most strongly the dangers of the Boston movement carry small informational brochures, called Intervention Instruments, which outline the activities and procedures of the Boston movement.

3. Attempts to find campus "respectability" through recognition as a student group.
Many campuses have brought sanctions against the activities of the Boston Church. I know of twenty-five or more that

have taken actions of one sort or another. Some, like Boston College, a Jesuit institution, just four miles from Boston University, simply announced that the Boston Church was not allowed on campus. In other cases, policy and administration leaders have drafted clear sets of behavioral standards, which are careful not to touch on questions of personal religious belief. Since the Boston Church has continually proved unwilling or unable to abide by the standards set for all religious organizations on the Boston University campus, it has been officially removed.

In recent years, however, in many cases the campus branch of the ICC has attempted to gain official recognition as a campus religious organization. One such attempt on the Boston University campus came through a young man who told me seriously that he wanted to organize a "new religious group" on the campus. When I asked the name or denomination of the group, he responded: "The ICCSO." We live by acronym, so I guessed that those initials referred to the International Churches of Christ Student Organization. He was surprised that I recognized the true identity of his organization so easily, and more surprised when I recited their long history on the campus, a history that he already knew perfectly well. This small duplicity along with the decision that the activities of the ICC had never changed since the days of 1988 caused it to be rejected again.

There is another approach that has been taken in several schools. A member of the church will apply for a position of authority, such as a Resident Assistant in a dormitory, a peer counselor in a college, or for the office of financial assistance. It is clearly illegal to ban students from such positions because of their religious beliefs or denominational affiliation. It is very justified, however, to require that no one use such a position to pressure prospective church members. A Teaching Assistant in the Physics Department was summarily dismissed some years ago, when he invited the students whom he was to grade to dinner at his apartment, then introduced them to church leaders who engaged in a Bible Talk and recruitment session. Such abuses of position are much easier to spot and deal with than the case of student workers in the cafeteria food line, who scold students coming for breakfast for not attending a meeting the evening before.

The student organization of the Boston Church has been recognized at a few campuses—very few. In every case I know of, the responsible administrators have come to regard decisions that were made on the church's pleas for fairness to be always destructive. The leaders of the groups involved will always respond that they did not understand the rules that were broken, or that the "enthusiasm" of new converts was just too great to contain.

4. Threats of legal action are seen and felt in many places.

In January 1994 I received a phone call from someone in London who said that he was a former member of the London Church of Christ. Since members of that organization had mentioned that I was an adversary, he said he wanted me to know that the Boston Church was about to sue Boston University and me for denying their rights to full and free access to our campus. I join most clergy who are totally innocent in knowledge of the law and legal procedures in such cases. But I immediately alerted our corporation counsel of this information.

Critical Perspectives

We waited for several months, then the office of the Dean of Students received a number of letters of complaint from members of the Church which alleged that they had been discriminated against, and harassed by me and certain other administrators and student leaders. The Dean's office set about instantly to check each allegation. None of them proved to have any foundation in fact. Several weeks later I was appearing at the University of Massachusetts to speak on the dangers of destructive religious activities, and the Dean at that university showed me exactly the same set of letters. Only the names had been changed to apply to the local situation.

My address at UMass was videotaped, since we knew that a large number of the members of the Boston movement would be in the audience. Following the address, the university received a formal and ominous request for a copy of the video for possible legal actions. Nothing ever came of the threats and I had nearly forgotten them.

Then, after six months had passed, I was speaking to Roman Catholic campus ministers in the New England area and reported the apparent threats of legal actions. Much to my surprise, I found that I had to get into a long line of universities who were completely and totally convinced that they were the ones who were to be the focus of legal action by the Boston Church.

I am greatly comforted by the confident affirmation of the legal department of our university that there is nothing that we have done or that I have said that puts us in any legal jeopardy. I am equally convinced, however, that the Boston movement is using these veiled threats of legal actions to shake some positive responses from university administrations who are reluctant to allow them admission to the university as recognized religious groups.

5. The walk-aways from the group are the remaining tragedy.

The greatest single change that has occurred since 1988 is the large and ever-increasing number of persons who are walking away from the Boston movement, emotionally exhausted and religiously confused. Some few persons have experienced some exit counseling which has brought them back into meaningful and realistic relationships with their families; a few have even been able to take what seems like a terrifying risk of talking to another clergyperson. But many have simply walked away disillusioned by deceit, hypocrisy, and the rigid, authoritarian control.

In some cases, students are able to cope in some aspects of their lives. Some can study adequately, but are severely handicapped in forming strong and trusting personal relationships. Their sense of self-worth has been totally flattened, and they have lost trust for most of the people around.

The problem is magnified by the scarcity of adequately trained psychologists who are able to work with the devastating effects of thought reform, particularly when combined with the theological language and religious structures of this religious organization. I have talked to many persons who confess tremendous relief to be free of the organizational weight put upon them by the ICC. They are organization free, and intellectually no longer bound by the coercive techniques. But many of these persons tell me that they still waken in the night with flashbacks of the dread that the pressure of the organization caused them, or the deeply ingrained emotional feeling that they are eternally damned because they have left the group. The emotional toll of ex-members is a fearful fact of our religious climate.

There are very few adequate support groups that can nurture such persons back to an emotional health, and some degree of religious security. One of my greatest concerns is that many persons who try to help ex-members have such a total contempt for the religious practices they have seen, that they enjoy engaging in simple "religion bashing." They do not recognize the power and support of healthy, constructive religious faith. One of the important tasks of clergy who will deal with ex-members is to find adequate ways of rebuilding trust with those who have been so seriously damaged by these religious practices.

Conclusion

It is now seventeen years since the first student group from the Lexington (now Boston) Church of Christ came to me asking to have a meeting in the University Chapel. I still remember that on that first occasion they lied to me, in a rather small way, about what they were doing and how they were doing it. I have heard many times since then that they do not believe that "a devil" deserves to have an even break, or even to be dealt with honestly. That continues to make any further relationships with the leadership of the group difficult.

At the end of the day I take some comfort in an historical insight that this group bears in its organization the seeds of its own destruction. This insight comes from knowing about a religious cult that was all-pervasive on the Italian peninsula, in and around Rome, in the first century, when the apostle Paul was probably imprisoned there for proclaiming the Christian faith. The group was the Cult of Mythra, an

43

adaptation of an Egyptian deity. The remains of one of their gathering places have been excavated at Ostia. The group grew to engulf a large number of the citizenry of first-century Rome and its environs. It is estimated that 85 to 90 percent of the citizens were involved with the group. Those figures even exceed Kip McKean's modest boast that he has converted more persons that did Saint Paul.

Yet, as I speak to student groups, few if any of them have ever heard of the Cult of Mythra. The reason is simple, according to the best authorities who have studied it. First, the group demanded absolute theological orthodoxy. No question or dissent was ever allowed. Second, all of its wealth and concern flowed in, and nothing went out to meet the needs of the world outside. Those two descriptions fit the Boston movement perfectly and completely.

At this moment, the movement is very strong and has exerted tremendously destructive power over many people. But there is the power in the creative spirit which God puts within each of us that simply cannot be contained by such authoritarian control. The spirit will break out to make us free.

Part II

Former Members Tell Their Stories

3

A Mental Health Approach

Lorna Goldberg and William Goldberg

We are clinical social workers who have been working with families of current and former members of cults and destructive groups since the 1970s. Typically, membership in these groups has hurt both the member and his or her family.

Recruits and new members are manipulated to accept a new set of attitudes, behaviors, alliances, and values that meet the needs of the group and its leader rather than provide something beneficial for the member. Individuals are hurt because their options are narrowed as they are cut off from familiar guideposts and induced to subjugate their own needs to those of the group.

Families in this situation become distraught, anxious, and confused as they observe sudden and drastic personality changes in their family member who is involved with such a group. Attempts to break through the veil of clichés, bland reassurances, and evasive answers are generally to no avail.

Our concern about these groups is aroused not because of the beliefs or doctrines. Instead, we focus on the unfair and manipulative recruitment techniques that induce fear and guilt, and narrow the options of those recruited. Once recruits become involved with the group, they develop a fear of leaving that is so profound that they equate leaving with being condemned to Hell.

Former members of the International Churches of Christ (ICC) have impressed us in numerous ways. Although they come from diverse backgrounds and a variety of cultural, ethnic, and racial groups, they share many personal characteristics. They are an exceptional group of young people: bright, idealistic, conscientious, and engaging. In fact, it is because of these very qualities that ICC reaches out to them. According to the jargon used by some in the group, these young people are "sharp." They were recruited by other "sharp" people who also possess strong and positive characteristics.

The former members who tell their stories in this section came from fairly religious backgrounds. They were not seekers by nature, although the idea of enhancing their spirituality and developing new friendships with seemingly like-minded people was appealing to them. Most were in a transitional life stage—for example, living in a new environment (often on a college campus). Joining a Bible study group appeared to be a safe and enriching way to make new friends.

Once initial contact with a recruiter was made, these young people found themselves swept along by the demands of the group. They did not wish to appear rude to peers, especially when being pressured to attend something as seemingly benign as a Bible study group. They became more involved because they had difficulty saying no (asserting themselves) to a religious group, and because they did not recognize the extent to which they were being manipulated.

The two of us have learned about ICC's practices primarily through our work. Unfortunately, many former members feel betrayed and burned by their experience with this group. Generally they describe initially having felt the positive effects of the flattering attention they were receiving, the friendships they were gaining, and the belief that they were serving God. But after they became members, eventually they found themselves pressured to spend all their time recruiting or finding ways to give more money to the group. Often members were sidetracked from previous goals, including educational achievements and career choices. They were pressured to serve the group full time and became alienated from their families and former friends. Over time, their initial excitement was replaced with despair and disillusionment.

For all the former members we've met, it took great courage to make the decision to leave. They were usually told by other members that leaving the group meant leaving God and thus as "fall aways" they would be condemned to Hell. With help, many former members have been able to see that the International Churches of Christ does not have the only interpretation of the Bible or of God's expectations. Some former ICC members have been able to return to their family's church or to begin to feel comfortable choosing another form of religious practice. Others, however, feel so deceived and manipulated by the experience that they have turned away from religion completely. This is one of the sad results of membership in this group and others like it.

Many former ICC members have not sought out either pastoral counseling or therapy. Since the discipling relationship, which is central to this group, is used as a way to control—that is, the discipling partner gives advice about everything and members learn to model themselves after their discipler in every way—it makes sense that a former member might tend to shy away from a new one-on-one or counseling relationship. Former cult members in general fear being manipulated, exploited, and deceived again.

Discipling partners are not really partners at all. There is no equality in the relationship. The discipler is there to be a guide in every matter of any consequence. The discipler's role is similar to that of a pastoral counselor or a psychotherapist in the sense that the disciple is encouraged to share intimate thoughts and feelings and look for guidance. Confidentiality, however, is rarely respected in the discipling relationship. And the actual goal is to tell members what to do rather than help them work out their own answers.

Although initially it may be frightening to contemplate religious and spiritual issues after such an experience, it is important for former ICC members to study the Bible with someone with theological expertise in order to gain a better understanding of different Bible interpretations. We also believe that exit counseling and/or therapy with a professional knowledgeable about cults can be helpful in sorting out and understanding the thought-reform aspects of the experience.

Those who leave without educating themselves about the group's manipulative practices may continue to blame themselves rather than the group for their need to leave. Often former members are filled with self-hatred, and play out these feelings through a variety of self-destructive behaviors. Once able to gain a fuller understanding of the destructive nature of the group, they are freed from the heavy burden of guilt and self-blame and can begin to have a fuller life, a life that contains many options and healthy goals.

The four accounts in this section are based on interviews conducted in 1993 and 1994. All of the individuals' names in this section are pseudonyms, and certain facts have been changed out of respect for privacy to the individuals and families involved. Since these interviews took place in New Jersey, the majority of the accounts are from the New York City Church of Christ, but we have found the experiences described here to be similar to those of ICC groups around the country. It appears that the church structure, doctrine, and authoritarian relationships are the same in every branch.

It is important to hear from people who were part of ICC because it may help others who are contemplating joining it or a similar group to consider all the consequences before getting too deeply involved. As the former members in this book attest, before they became fully immersed in the movement they were shown only a portion of the demands that would be made on them. As their involvement became more intense, more focused, and more time consuming, the definition of an acceptable commitment was changed. Instead of devoting one night a week plus Sunday, they were expected to devote two nights a week, then three, then more. Outside interests and activities had to be abandoned as members were induced to feel guilty about doing anything that took time away from their group activities. As they displayed a willingness to accede to the escalating demands, those demands were, in turn, increased.

We believe strongly that individuals in a free society have the right to join any organizations they wish. However, we also believe that individuals should understand what will happen to them after they join, so that they can make an informed decision about joining. Our hope is that the accounts that follow will help potential members make an informed choice about their future.

4

"I Decided to Attend the Bible Study..."

James Ash
(As Told to William Goldberg)

My first encounter with the New York City Church of Christ occurred when I was a college student. I was working as a busboy in a restaurant during my summer vacation and one of the waiters was in the group. He invited me to study the Bible with him. I told him that I really had no religion, that I had gone to church a total of two times in my life. Nevertheless, I was interested in developing my spiritual side. At the time I was reading complex philosophical novels, trying to find my spiritual and moral center. I decided to attend the Bible study.

I felt that the person leading the discussion was trying to do the right thing. I'm a musician and he was one too. The people in the group kept asking me to participate in activities like picnics, musical events, and church services. I ended up accepting these invitations even though I didn't have much time because I was spending most of my time practicing my instrument.

They were pretty persistent, but at the same time I liked their friendship. I really didn't want to do all the things they were asking of me, but I didn't want to hurt their feelings. If they had stopped calling, I never would have called them; but when I didn't have anything else to do, I went along with them. After an activity, they'd say, "Let's do this again," and we'd make a date. I thought they were just being friendly, but now I realize that they were manipulating me.

In the Bible study, I didn't accept everything they said. They said, for example, that the Bible was not open to interpretation, that there was only one possible interpretation. I felt pretty uncomfortable about that. Also some of the leaders sounded pretty arrogant. One in particular bothered me because I felt that he was insincere and arrogant. At first I disliked him; but after I joined the group, I convinced myself that I loved him like a brother. I thought I was overcoming my prejudice because he was a Southerner and I'm black.

Back in school after the summer, I stopped reading the Bible and found that I was feeling guilty about it. When someone from the New York City Church of Christ started a Bible discussion on my campus, I was happy to join. I was beginning to miss the group. I was lonely.

I studied with two other fellows, and they started putting pressure on me to come to the church. I really wasn't interested. After a while when they couldn't get to me in other ways, they gave me a "three-week challenge." In order to meet the challenge, I was asked to come to church for three weeks, three times each week. They make it seem like so little, but I really didn't have much time between school and my music. I agreed to take the challenge because I didn't want to be impolite. They seemed so sincere, as though they really wanted to help me.

When they felt that I was listening to them, the people in the church started pressuring me to get baptized. They told me that if I got hit by a car tomorrow, I'd go straight to Hell.

I didn't totally believe that, but I admit that I noticed I began to feel uneasy crossing streets.

After the baptism I was happy for a few months, but then I had to push myself to keep up the smile. I noticed things that bothered me. For example, one of the other people in the church was a talented artist. He was under so much pressure to participate in group activities that he completely ignored his artwork. He told me that he didn't care because he had found God. His talent was going to waste and it didn't even bother him.

Even though I was supposed to, I didn't talk about the church to everybody I met. I'm basically a shy person, so I felt uncomfortable approaching strangers. The people in the church told me that my shyness was a sin when it came to doing church business, so I started forcing myself to speak to a few people a week. The church was taking up more and more of my time and I began neglecting my musical practice.

I had been told that I was supposed to have been committed to the church before I was baptized, but I knew that I really hadn't been that committed. I started to feel guilty because I thought that God would know that in my heart, I hadn't been sincere. It bothered me more and more and eventually I couldn't sleep at night. I was in terror of going to Hell. It was the worst time in my life. I had gone from feeling great to feeling okay to feeling poorly to feeling terrible. By my senior year of college, I started to break down. I couldn't stop looking at women, and that was considered lustful by the church. I developed a tic. I couldn't collect my thoughts.

I started noticing that the leaders of the church were leading a lifestyle that was pretty extravagant while the rest of us were sacrificing. As time went on I found it more and more impossible to be happy. By my senior year I was reading the Bible two and a half to four hours a day to get over what they called my "spiritual war." I prayed at least an hour every day. I didn't have time or concentration for other things. I didn't realize that it was the guilt and isolation that had created my problems, so I tried to solve them by becoming more guilty and isolated.

The leaders told me not to talk to other members about my struggles. They said it was because they didn't want others to have to struggle in the same way, but I know now that it was because other people would acknowledge that they had similar pain, doubts, and fears.

After I graduated I was encouraged to move out of my parents' apartment, so I moved in with some others from the church. Meanwhile, my tic got worse and I was fired from my job. Now I had even fewer outside influences.

Once I was attracted to a woman in the church, and she was clearly interested in me. One of my roommates who was higher in the church hierarchy liked her too. Another leader told me that I shouldn't develop a relationship with the woman because I wasn't spiritually ready for it yet. He told me that I wasn't even getting along with my roommate, so how could I have a relationship with a woman? My roommate ended up marrying the woman.

The next summer I had a wonderful opportunity. I was asked to teach at a music camp. I would make good money plus room and board. Of course, it would mean that I couldn't be a part of the church that summer. When my church leaders heard about it, they told me that I had better pray about it before I accepted the position. My discipling partner told me that he'd support any decision I made after I had engaged in earnest prayer over it. I prayed and decided that

I would go, but I'd return to the city during my one break and would go to church then. I was told that I had obviously not prayed hard enough, and that I would have to draw up a plan so that I could come back more often. I presented that to the camp directors, and they told me that I had to stay there for the entire summer. I didn't want to miss this opportunity, so I accepted the camp's terms.

When I went back to my discipling partner and told him about my decision, he got very upset. He told me that I was risking my salvation by working at the camp. In retrospect, I realize that kind of attitude on my discipler's part was part of the deception. He had originally said that he'd support any decision I made. It turned out that he'd only support the decision he wanted me to make.

I decided that rather than risk my salvation I wouldn't go to the music camp. Now my parents got upset because I was passing up such a great opportunity. My discipling partner asked me to tell others about my decision at a Bible Talk and I did. Instead of praising me for making the "right" decision, though, he said that it wasn't a "pure" decision because I had been talked into not going. It wasn't from my heart. I felt used and betrayed. I was furious, but I wasn't able to express my anger because I had been taught to submit. But I started thinking about leaving.

Someone must have sensed that I was unhappy because Ken, one of the leaders, started reaching out to me. I thought that we were becoming friends, but after a little while he handed me off to someone else. I guess that's part of the hypocrisy. Friendship is used as a tool to keep people in. It isn't sincere.

After the fallout about my working at the camp, I started to rebel in quiet ways. I asked women from outside the church for dates. I skipped some services. For a while, I enjoyed the freedom, then I started to feel guilty and depressed. I was angry that they'd been discouraging me from practicing my musical instrument, one of the things that gave me pleasure.

I started to recognize that there was a destructive element in the group. I wanted to leave, but I had been told that my life would fall apart if I did. One day I went out on a date with another member. She started telling me how angry she was. She was a talented artist but felt stifled in her personal and professional life because of the church. I knew that I felt the same way. I didn't go to services for the next two weeks. Instead, I concentrated on practicing. I was pretty productive during those two weeks. Even my music teacher noticed how much better I was doing. He told me that if I would practice like that all the time, I'd be much more successful. Now that really got me wondering! The church people had told me that if I attended all the services and just let God take over, my career would soar.

Even though I was having these doubts, I started feeling guilty and depressed because I wasn't going to services. I thought that maybe they were right, so I decided to try again. It was around that time that I was assigned a new discipling partner. I mentioned to him that I was going on vacation with my parents. He told me that he had checked with one of the higher-ups and that I had been given permission to go. I hadn't been asking his permission! I was just telling him my plans.

When I got back from the vacation, I met with my new discipling partner and told him that I wasn't coming back to the church. He asked me if I was happy with this decision and I told him I was. He said to me, "You think you're happy?"

and "You think you're talented?"—both in a condescending, imperious manner. I never went to services again.

It's been a year and a half since I left the church. The biggest problem I've had was coming to grips with the fact that the deep friendships I supposedly had while in the church weren't real. The others really weren't interested in me. I know that because no one with whom I was friendly while I was in the group is interested in renewing the friendship now that I'm out.

My phobias are basically gone, and my tic is gone. My musical career is going quite well. It's been a renaissance for me. I've gotten in touch with my real feelings. I'm growing personally and professionally. While I was in, I had stagnated. Everyone says I'm like a different person now, and I like the person I am.

5

"I Thought She Was Just Being Friendly..."

Sally Young
(As Told to William Goldberg)

I was born in an East Coast city. My father was a pharmacist in Jamaica and managed a fish store when he moved to the United States in the late fifties. My mother is from Georgia. I attended public schools. When I was fifteen years old, my parents separated.

I graduated from an Ivy League university in 1990 with a degree in English. I am earning a master's degree and now work for a large-circulation periodical writing promotional material.

I was first approached by a representative from the New York City Church of Christ in 1991 while talking with my best friend, Dina, at the college student center. We were both complaining about the difficulties we were having with our boyfriends and another young woman said, "I know exactly what you're talking about." She said that she also had boyfriend problems and we started to chat. My girlfriend was suspicious of this stranger who joined in our conversation uninvited, but I thought she was just being friendly so I gave her my telephone number.

THE BOSTON MOVEMENT

Two days later she called me; in the midst of the conversation, she asked me if I believed in God and if I had a church. It happens that although I was raised Episcopalian, I was not comfortable with my church and was looking for a new one that better met my needs. I was feeling guilty and confused at the time because I had been involved with another man and had to choose between him and my boyfriend, Drew. I was looking for a way to structure my life. When the young woman asked me if I would like to study the Bible with her, I thought that the study might help me to clear up the confusion. I've always been a friendly person who gets along with all kinds of people, and I thought that there could be nothing wrong with studying the Bible, so I agreed.

The woman/recruiter met me at my job and studied with me and a group of others from her church. It wasn't the Bible study that hooked me, it was the people involved in the study. They all seemed to understand my dilemma. Some of them said that they had experiences similar to mine. They said they would listen to me, that I could call them at any time. In short order, I decided that I wanted to be a part of this friendly group, so I joined their church.

My friends and family noticed a big change in me. I was drifting away from Drew and Dina. They felt that I was becoming cold and distant. My mother started complaining that I was getting home at one or two in the morning almost every night. I tried to explain to her that I had important meetings for my church and that my soul was more important than my family or my sleep. The people from the church told me that my mother was trying to control me and that I shouldn't let her. She couldn't understand the necessity of attending church functions. I was converted to the church within a week; at the end of three months, I was made a Bible Talk leader.

In retrospect I realize that the ceremony at which I made my 100-percent commitment to the church was contrived and manipulated. It was very dramatic. During the seventh of nine studies, when I was particularly vulnerable, I was suddenly asked if I would like to go to Heaven or Hell. It was at that point that I "snapped" and proclaimed myself a true believer in the church. I was willing to do anything they asked of me because I wanted to go to Heaven.

Church meetings began to monopolize my time. Meetings were held several evenings a week and on Sundays. The evening meetings began at 8 p.m. We would sing and then would have to list all the people we spoke to that day and whether we were able to convert them. Every time I saw someone during the day I knew I would have to try to approach that person because I would have to answer to the church leaders if I let the opportunity go by. I was not able to leave the meetings until 11 p.m.; by the time I got home, it would be midnight. My mother was becoming more and more upset.

I have a physical disability that requires monitoring, but I continued to travel to the meetings. I was told that Satan was attacking me physically to keep me from joining the church and that my mother's objections were because she didn't want me to be saved. I kept working on my mother and, finally, after several months, she came to a meeting and said that she had joined the church. I still don't know whether she joined to appease me or because she was really converted.

Meanwhile, Dina and Drew were becoming more upset. They saw that I was distant and always exhausted. Drew told Dina that it was clear to him that I was involved in a cult. My elders in the church told me to stop seeing him because he only wanted me for sex. Within a few months I had left my boyfriend, cut off ties with most of my nonchurch friends, and had no time for my family. The church people told me that it was my obligation to save my friends from going to Hell, so I worked on them constantly and brought nine people into the church, including my mother, my sister, and Dina.

I was told that I had to approach at least ten people each day and bring at least two new recruits into the church each week. I started to feel like a pharisee, someone more interested in show than in the reality of spirituality. I felt that all I was doing was trying to meet my quota of converts and had lost sight of God.

The final straw was when Michael (one of the church members) came on to Dina in a sexual way. I remembered a passage from Corinthians that said that if your bother is immoral, you should lead him to God. I called one of the church leaders and told her how upset I was over Michael's immoral actions. She put me on hold for five minutes; I knew that she was getting advice from her husband about how to "handle" me. When she got back on the phone, she said that Michael was not being immoral, he was just having impure thoughts, and that her husband would speak to him. I felt betrayed, as if there were a double standard operating.

The next week my friend Will, who was a member of the church, told me he had to speak to me. Will said that he had found out that the leaders were wealthier than they pretended to be and that he had proof of property they owned. I was upset because I had been told that we were not helping homeless people because we did not have enough money, but the leaders owned property.

Here I was giving 10 percent of my net income and I didn't see us helping poor people. Where was all the money going? At first I was confused, but then I realized that I had been fooled. I joined the church for spiritual reasons, but spent most of my time pressuring people to join. I thought that we would be helping poor people, but I never saw this happen. I thought that I would become a better Christian, but ended up alienating my friends.

I started telling all the people that I had brought in about my doubts and the discrepancies I saw. I called Dina, who was vacationing in Hawaii, and told her that I had decided to leave. I had to get to her before the church did because I knew they would try to turn her against me. Luckily, Dina's respect and affection for me were strong enough that she listened to me, as did my mother and sister.

Once the church leaders found out I had left, a meeting was called and everyone was told that I was under Satan's influence. These people, who a week earlier had thought that I was the greatest thing in the world, now said that they had seen signs all along that I was not really a good church member. They said I was a spy from the beginning and that I sat in meetings just so I could pull people out of the church. They said I was a liar. I was so hurt and depressed because I had joined the church for sincere spiritual reasons.

Since I left I feel that I'm in control of my life again. I married Drew and thank God the church was not able to destroy my feelings for him. I have found a new relationship with God, one that is based on real spirituality and not on fear, exploitation, and manipulation. Since I left the church, I'm once again free.

6

"On My Second Day in the Dorms, I Was Approached..."

Nina Cuong
(As Told to Lorna Goldberg)

I was born in Southeast Asia in 1973. My family came to the United States as refugees when I was three years old and eventually we settled in Connecticut, after living in a refugee camp in Arkansas for several months. My mother became a born-again Christian when I was about seven. I was raised in the Baptist church and was baptized at thirteen. My father was a Buddhist; he also studied the Bible for a while, but eventually stopped. My parents separated for a time when I was about six, but they got back together after my mother became a Christian.

I had an older brother, but he died two years ago in a car accident. He had been drinking and his car smashed into a tree. When it happened, I was already in the group; in fact, it was the only time that the women's counselor, who was leading the campus ministry, ever returned my call. She called to make sure that I was aware that my brother was in Hell since he had never become a "disciple" of the New York City Church of Christ. My brother had, however, professed to believe in Christ and had been baptized when he was about twelve, although he may not have been living the "Christian life" at the time of his death. Only God can judge what my brother's eternal destiny is. I was so brainwashed and out of touch with reality that I accepted what the women's counselor told me without question, and even repeated to my mother what I was told to believe.

My brother's death came as a shock to me, and it was only months later that the impact began to hit me. A slow healing process had only begun as I learned to deal with the grief and the loss. To the credit of some of the people in the group—the majority of whom I believe are good, sincere people who truly love God and want to serve Him, but are sadly misled—I must add that two of the "sisters" from the group came home with me to support me and my family during my brother's funeral. They were a great comfort to me.

While I was growing up, my father was a restaurant worker, then a mechanic; for the past ten years, he's been a factory worker. He had been a teacher in our native country and then an officer in its army. He was able to get his associate's degree shortly after coming to the United States. My mother has worked as a secretary and bank clerk. She is presently working part-time and going to college. She speaks English fluently and is doing well in her classes. I'm very proud of both my parents for their hard work and perseverance through difficult times. They now own a house in Connecticut and are doing quite well for themselves, especially considering the fact that they were refugees less than twenty years ago.

I went to church a lot while I was growing up and spent summers at a Christian camp. These were very positive experiences for me. When I became a staff member at the camp, I noted some hypocrisy among the staff. They would tell dirty jokes and watch dirty movies. That hypocrisy troubled me.

I worked hard in school and graduated third in my class. I was the feature editor of the school newspaper and won two awards for journalism. I was also elected president of the Interact Club, the junior branch of the Rotary Club. I won a Rotary Club scholarship to college, as well as a full, four-year tuition/dorm scholarship from the Alumni Scholarship and Welfare Fund of the school to which I had applied. I had thought about going to a Christian college, but the students weren't that friendly at the ones I visited. Also, I didn't have enough money to be able to turn down a full scholarship offer.

I was excited about college and living in the dorms, but I also wanted to have a church affiliation. On my second day in the dorms I was approached by my resident assistant, Cindy, and her friend Kate. They were both disciples in the New York City Church of Christ, although I didn't know it at the time. When I asked Kate if she knew of a good church in the area, she invited me to come with them to church on Sunday.

When I arrived at their church, I was impressed by seeing so many young, good-looking, and enthusiastic college students praying and singing together. The students looked so appealing, especially one college student who caught my eye. I hadn't dated a lot of boys in high school because I had wanted to date a Christian. That day the preaching brought tears to my eyes. It was almost overwhelming to feel so emotional.

After the service a young woman asked me if I wanted to study the Bible with her. I had a week before school classes started, so I agreed. Although I had studied the Bible all my life, I had never studied it as hard as I did that week. After the first study, one of the girls studying with me asked me how I could call myself a Christian when I didn't seem "broken about the cross of Jesus." I had heard about the cross all my life and it didn't send me into a fit of tears every time someone mentioned it, but now I thought maybe she had a point.

Initially, it was a bit difficult for the church members to convince me that I wasn't already a Christian, but I wanted so much to be a part of the group that I was willing to agree to anything they said. I tried to make myself believe it. I was impressed with how well they all seemed to know the Bible. We studied verses and made connections that I had never quite seen before or hadn't known enough about to contradict. Each study session was like a great revelation to me, and I felt ecstatic to be enlightened along with them. They had more knowledge and seemed to have a closer relationship to God than I did. It took only a week for them to convert me.

The next Sunday Brad, the cute guy I had seen at my first meeting, came up to me and said, "I hear you're getting baptized tonight. I'll announce it next Wednesday night at service." I was thrilled that he was even talking to me. The future looked bright.

After I was baptized I told my parents that I had joined a new church and that until you're baptized in this church, you're not a true Christian. I told them they were going to Hell. My mother was alarmed and had me see our old pastor. He showed me different Bible interpretations and said that in five years I'd be out of the church, burnt out from the demands placed on me. He managed to plant seeds of doubt in my mind about the group, but on the surface I scorned him because I felt that he didn't have Scriptures as readily on hand as members of the group did. Plus, I still had clear recollections of the hypocrisy that I had seen within his church while I was growing up. But mainly, I was so excited to have found such an enthusiastic and seemingly happy group of young believers that I was unwilling to let anyone try to dissuade me. Discovering the group seemed to be the answer to my prayers for just such a church; it seemed that God had led me to them.

I returned to the church and continued to be infatuated with Brad. He was twenty-five and I was eighteen. It soon became apparent that he just wanted to be friends, but that was all right. I was dating a lot in the church and making many good friends.

I eventually met Joshua, who asked me to go steady. Although we liked each other, there was church pressure against our relationship. They felt that I was putting my relationship with him before my obedience to the church. I was told that I needed to date someone who was a leader. Joshua had everything it took to be a powerful leader, but he always seemed to have a lot of doubts about the church.

I was sold on the church, but I also loved Joshua so I could never fully give up his friendship. We were so attracted to each other that we were always afraid of "falling into sin" with each other. Twice we were harshly rebuked for French kissing. The constant strain of everyone disapproving of and monitoring our relationship was too much for me. Eventually, Joshua and I were forced to break up.

By this time I was becoming a leader. Since I'm a friendly person, I was pretty good at recruiting; as a result, I was given more responsibility in the church. However, I was stressed out all the time between the demands of school, work, and the church. I no longer had time to date or speak with friends. I had to "serve" the church and I was so busy trying to recruit people or being involved in meetings or child care that I had no time for a relationship or even friendships.

I also had no time to think. If I disagreed with something about the church, I was told that I was "prideful." I was sure that the top leaders could see right through me and all my supposed sins. The leaders were so harsh. They pulled me in with love, then ruled over me with an iron fist.

I was miserable seeing Joshua date other people. I had to put on a happy face and act phony. I was even re-baptized hoping to regain my joy in the church. It didn't seem to work. I finally decided that I would leave the church. Since I was told that I would fall headlong into sin if I left the church, I telephoned Joshua and told him that I wanted to have sex with him, but I changed my mind at the last moment. I felt really miserable.

Naturally I confessed what I had done because I wanted to remain in the church. I was nearly disfellowshipped for it. But the leaders decided to give me another chance, except that my heart just could not find any peace or contentment in being with the church. I was finally told to take some time off, to "get my heart right with God." When I tried to come back, I was told, "You can't come back until God wants you back—if He wants you back."

I was terribly shaken. I didn't want to go to Hell, but I knew I couldn't make a commitment to a church I had no heart for. I also was told that I needed to take more time away from the church, and that I wasn't to talk to anyone in the church until I was "restored." I think they were trying to break my spirit, and they almost succeeded.

At first, I felt a bit relieved at not being under all the stress that I had experienced before; yet, at the same time, I was terribly lonely and depressed. It felt as though my world had dropped out from under me. All my closest friends were in the church, and now they couldn't talk to me. I had to start all over. I felt broken emotionally, like my faith had been delivered a nearly fatal blow. I didn't know whom or what to believe anymore.

I saw my life go from bad to worse. I felt seriously tempted to do things that I never would have done before I became a part of the group, such as having a one-night stand with a total stranger or getting completely drunk. Fortunately, I didn't do such things, but I came dangerously close a few times. I had been told that terrible things happened to people who left the church; the leaders said that those people had left God and had turned to Satan.

My life suddenly seemed like a self-fulfilling prophecy. Now I see it as a natural reaction to having been spiritually and emotionally raped and abused in a deceitful and manipulative manner. At any rate, I knew I needed help. I decided to return to a Baptist church and try to sort out my life and rebuild my faith.

I started attending a Baptist church, which helped me a great deal. I made several very good friends my own age who were serious about their faith and tried to live it out as best as they could. Those friendships were truly a blessing. I also talked to one of the assistant pastors in the church, who explained to me that the International Churches of Christ (ICC) misinterprets Scripture. Through the Baptist church, I found out about a group of former ICC members. They confirmed a lot of my suspicions about the manipulation used in the ICC.

I went to see Joshua with information about the church. He investigated my sources, had the information confirmed, and then also decided to leave the church. I am thankful to God for that. Joshua continued to investigate the church for more than a month after he left, discovering even more information. Now we are both convinced that it is a hypocritical and manipulative group.

If God had not used my relationship with Joshua to get me to leave the group, I would still be caught up in it. My experience in the New York City Church of Christ was definitely one of spiritual and emotional abuse. Instead of loving God, I feel that the leaders of the church became my gods. I had to follow them without question. The Baptist church I belong to now is helping me to love God the way I used to.

7

"They Said I Could Meet
Some Other Musicians There..."

Edgar Vann
(As Told to William Goldberg)

I am a twenty-five-year-old African living in the Northeast. I was born in Africa and lived there until I was ten years old, when I moved to England. My father is a civil engineer and my mother is a businesswoman. I moved to New England in 1986 to go to college. I am now a musician and composer.

I first encountered the New York City Church of Christ while walking on Broadway on the upper west side of Manhattan. A young woman came up to me and we started talking. She seemed friendly and I didn't have too many friends since I had just moved there. After we talked for a while, she told me that a group of friends got together to study the Bible and she asked me if I were free that night. I grew up as a Roman Catholic, but I hadn't gone to church in years. However, I still believed in the Bible. When she mentioned the Bible, I was neither turned on nor turned off. I'm still not sure whether I agreed to go with her because she convinced me that this would be a good use of my time or because I wanted to get to know her better.

Once I got to the Bible study class, I met a fellow named Lewis. He had also lived in England, so I felt a kinship with him. The people there were nice, but there was an air about the place that made me uncomfortable. They were *too* nice. They were trying too hard. It just didn't seem real, and I felt that they were up to something.

At the end of the Bible discussion they asked me for my phone number. I gave it to them because I thought we could be friends. Every time they called, though, they asked me to come to another Bible study. Finally, I agreed because they were so persistent and because I didn't want to be rude. I thought to myself, "What could be the harm in studying the Bible?" I agreed to go to another meeting.

Again I felt glad to be with friendly people in a new city, but I was uncomfortable with how overly friendly they were. They told me there were a lot of musicians in the group and invited me to the place where they had services. They said I could meet some of the other musicians there.

After the service at the theater a lot of people swarmed over me. It turned out that all of them were musicians. Every person who might have any kind of connection with me came over. I felt that it was contrived, but I wanted to meet people in the music business.

I knew that we had different goals. They were trying to recruit me and I was trying to make contacts. I wasn't sure that this was the best way to advance my career, so I decided to go my own way. When I moved to a new apartment I decided not to give these sincere but what I considered zealous church members my new number.

A year later I was working on the street, trying to get people to subscribe to a newspaper. I met a young woman who said she would sign up if I agreed to come to her church.

We joked about it. I didn't respond about the church but I did give her my number because I thought we might be friends. She started calling me, using the same arguments that I had heard the year before. She kept asking me to attend a service and, one day, I finally agreed.

When I got to the church, I met Lewis again. It was then that I realized that it was the same church from the year before. Lewis said to me, "See how God works! He brought you back!" Actually, I was glad to see him. He was a nice guy and it felt good to see someone I knew. We exchanged phone numbers, and he started calling me a lot—almost every day. When he invited me to a Bible study, I agreed to go. After all, he was a nice guy, and I thought that if he was in the group, it had to be okay. He and I had so many things in common.

At the Bible discussions I met other people who were close to my age. Everyone seemed young and happy. After the Bible discussion people would hang out and talk. They were like a family and it seemed harmless.

After a while Lewis told me that it would help me if I went to individual Bible study, and I agreed. There would be three of us there: Lewis, me, and another person who would take notes for me. I would have preferred to take my own notes, but they explained that this way I could concentrate on the teachings. I didn't realize that if they supplied the note taker, I would have notes only on what they deemed to be important. There would be no part of me in it. Also, by having two people there, they could "double team" me.

At these sessions, I would read a passage from the Bible, then I'd give my interpretation of it. Lewis would then tell me the "right" interpretation and the note taker would back him up. There was no room for another point of view. Despite this fact, I still felt that it was benign. After a few sessions they started coming to my apartment and pressuring me. After each session, no matter when I said I'd see them again, they tried to get me to come sooner. I had other commitments, though, and I was resistant to their pressure. I wanted to study the Bible, but only once a week.

After a while Lewis's attitude toward me changed. One day he got real angry. He said to me, "Edgar, you're really pushing me. You're like a brother to me and I want to save your soul. If I have to use physical violence to get you to come more often, I will." Once when I had missed a session he said, "I've been doing all this for you and this is how you repay me?" He started putting more and more pressure on me. Finally, in desperation, he said that he wanted me to speak to an elder in the church.

At first the elder was nice. He liked the kinds of things that I liked. I felt that we had a lot in common. Then he got serious. He said to me, "Edgar, how do you feel about your life? If I draw your life out on a continuum, where would you be according to the Scripture? If you died now, would you go to Heaven or to Hell?" I was beginning to soften. He demanded to know whether I was in light or darkness. I said that I was in between, and I started to get scared about what he was saying. I wanted to be saved. I had always thought of myself as a good person, but now I started to think of myself as a sinner. After four hours of intense pressure, I was broken down. I said that I wanted to be saved and that I would change my life.

The next day Lewis called and I went right over. I told him I knew I was a sinner and I needed to repent, but I still felt uncomfortable joining the church because I knew I had been pressured and I wasn't being myself. Lewis said that he was frightened about what might happen to me. What if I left today and something happened to me? I would go straight to Hell. I was scared and confused. I finally told him I would join the church. Lewis immediately made a phone call and made arrangements to save my soul. I was baptized in a bathtub in August 1990.

Everyone was so happy for me, and I was happy for myself. I knew I had made the right decision. But after four days the euphoria began to wear off. I was told that I should move in with brothers from the church. I didn't really want to, but they worked on me for another month and finally I agreed.

Once I moved into the apartment, I found myself answering to the church for everything I did. Each day I would have to explain my actions, how I had used my time, to whom had I talked, and whether I had won any new converts for the church.

I was convinced that this was the True Church, but now and then I felt restricted and like there was something wrong. For example, I had a friendship with one of the sisters in the group and we used to talk on the phone a lot. Lewis and my friend's discipling partner told us we were getting too close, that we must stop spending so much time together. I didn't like that, but Lewis said I was just being rebellious. He asked me whether Jesus would talk to a girl late every night on the telephone. He told me that I was hurting her spiritually. I didn't have an answer for that.

One New Year's Eve I went out to a club and took some church members with me. When Lewis found out about it, he got angry. He bawled me out and told me that I was making those people stumble. I felt that he was more of a Christian than I was and that he must be right. I vowed to live like a true Christian and started spending all my free time trying to convert people. I began approaching strangers on the subway to get them to join the church.

After seven or eight months they decided I was ready for leadership meetings; so in June 1991 I became a Bible Talk leader. Once I had made the commitment, that was all I thought about. I still went to work because I had to make a living, but my mind was always on my Bible Talk. I was good at it, too. I learned how to "protect" people, to warn them not to speak to outsiders unless they could control the conversation. Every day I reported to my leaders about my productivity that day.

I was still performing, playing keyboard and singing, but the people in my band and in the audience were church members. Every other Saturday we threw a party in my apartment, for the purpose of recruiting new people and show them what a good time we had in the church. I realized that this was for show and I felt bad about it, but I felt that the good I got from being in the church outweighed the bad. I decided that the fact that I had so many friends outweighed the negatives. I accepted their reasoning that my disagreements with the church were just examples of my pride getting in the way of the Truth, that it was just legalism.

In February 1992 I was told that I was to run a second Bible Talk every week. By this time I had gotten close to the leadership. It seemed that as a leader you could get away with a lot of things. My heart wasn't in it like it had been before.

Then in April a church member left. Although I wasn't supposed to, I went to his apartment and asked him why he had left. He said, "I've learned a lot about this group," but was reluctant to go into more detail. I wanted to know what he meant, and he finally said, "The church makes a lot of money." It had crossed my mind that the leaders were living in nice apartments and traveled a lot. They seemed to have it made. I started noticing more and more. My friend's wife said to me, "Edgar, this group is after your money." I hated to admit it, but what she said seemed to be true.

I had been told not to speak to ex-members because they were "of the Devil," but I started speaking to some and asking them why they had left. They confirmed some of the things that I had noticed but hadn't let myself think about. Now I understood why we weren't supposed to talk to ex-members. Everything just came together and it became clearer and clearer.

Soon after this experience there was tremendous pressure on people to increase their tithe for that week. We were told that whatever we had been giving had to be increased twenty times. I was told that if someone in my group said they couldn't afford to do that, I should tell them to go without lunch so they could contribute more. I felt terrible about pressuring people in that way. We were told to kick people out who were unemployed and couldn't give money. It upset me that the leaders were living so well, while we were pressuring the regular members to give up so much.

One weekend I went to a nearby city with an ex-member to visit my brother. All the way there I asked him questions. I went to a local service and during the service, one of the leaders took out a twenty-dollar bill and said, "Money equals souls." Suddenly everything became clear to me. I knew I had to leave.

The ex-member to whom I had talked offered to let me stay with him and his wife for a while, so I moved my stuff out of the apartment I had been sharing with other members. The next day I was visited at my job by two church leaders. They kept asking me what happened, "Why did I decide to

78

leave? Whom did I talk to?" They told me that I was going to Hell. To get them off my back, I said that maybe I would reconsider. They were satisfied for the moment.

They started calling me all the time, using every trick they knew I had fallen for in the past. One day they showed up at my friend's apartment when I wasn't there. They barged in and said, "Where's Edgar? We've come to take him back!" When my friend finally convinced them that I wasn't there, they left—but first warned him that they'd be back.

I was really scared. For two or three weeks I was hiding from them. I thought they might physically injure me. Since I wasn't a citizen, I thought they could have me deported. They harassed my friend so much that I finally agreed to meet with them, but all they kept asking was what did I know and to whom had I spoken. I got in touch with AFF and they helped me contact an attorney who wrote them a letter. After that the church people backed off. They told other members to stay away from me because I was of the devil.

I feel now that my membership was just another life experience and I try to learn from it. A lot of people were hurt by the church. They have no self-esteem left. It feels great to be out. I've been able to get on with my life. When I meet church members on the street, I can see how close-minded most of them are. If they ask me questions, I tell them the truth. I give them facts and suggest some people to call. I feel good that I've helped some people to leave the group.

Part III

More Personal Experiences

8

Learning About Mind Control the Hard Way

Mary Sartorio

Dear God, In his eyes, he probably thinks that he is married to a member of a religious cult. I know that this cannot be further from the truth, but I cannot help feeling confused!

—Journal excerpt, June 1992

Before Tom and I were married, we formed a friendship with a couple from the New York City Church of Christ. While I was away at graduate school, my husband met Tod McKinley at his new job. They quickly developed a friendship that included playing basketball on the weekends in various parks throughout the city, enjoying long talks over lunch about books they'd each read, attending dinner parties, and working on Tod's new apartment. Throughout this friendship Tom and I were frequently invited by Tod to attend one of his church services at the Javits Center.

In the summer of 1990 we went to Tod's wedding, which was when I first met Tod and his wife, Joan. Without knowing it at the time, at the wedding we were surrounded by members of Tod and Joan's church. A couple of dinner dates later we accepted an invitation to an AIDS benefit at Symphony Space sponsored by the NYC Church of Christ. Much to my surprise, donations were not collected (although ticket prices were steep), attendance was multicultural, and the talent was obvious.

By this time I was intrigued by Tod and Joan's lifestyle and my curiosity about their church had skyrocketed. Their personal life was packed with dinner parties, meetings, and special events. I couldn't understand how one couple could have so many great friends, all from one church. What was the attraction? I was given the impression that their church was made up of young men and women from all backgrounds and that the church's primary interest was in benevolence. When my husband asked Tod which religion he and Joan were affiliated with and what their beliefs were, he was given vague answers. I was only able to conclude that it was not a mainstream religion.

Believing that Tod and Joan were more knowledgeable about theology than I, coupled with the fact that I was interested in deepening my relationship with God through the Bible, I felt comfortable speaking with Joan after the show. I mentioned to her my desire to learn more about the Bible. To me, the Bible was a textbook at best, which was somewhat bothersome to me since I claimed to be a Christian yet felt I didn't know enough about Jesus or the Bible. I felt like a hypocrite. It was during this conversation that Joan offered to buy me a Bible that was easy to read—and she did.

Another important incident occurred a few months after the concert. Tom met Tod in Manhattan for a Saturday afternoon of basketball. After playing Tom was invited to join Tod and his friends for pizza. The group walked to a pizzeria and had dinner together. Afterward Tod surprised Tom by asking him, loud enough to be heard by the entire group, if he wanted to study the Bible. Tom had never been interested in Tod's church. He had known Tod for more than a year and by now knew that Tod was extremely active in the Church of Christ. Frequently invited to services, Tom always politely declined, letting Tod know on a number of occasions that he, Tom, had no interest in the church. Even though he considered the devotion that Tod and his friends exhibited toward the church a bit excessive, Tom remained friends with Tod.

This occasion after the game was the first time Tom had been asked to read the Bible with them. Tom felt quite pressured, for not only were they in a public place but also he knew that the other two men were also members of the church. Not wanting to show any disrespect toward Tod or embarrass him in front of his friends, Tom replied, "Oh, I don't have a Bible." Tod quickly retorted, "You can use this one," and pulled out a spare Bible. Tom could only reply, "All right," and resigned himself to just follow along with their reading.

As Tod set up the reading, which was the account of the Crucifixion, Tom noticed that the other two were taking notes. One said, "Oh, don't worry, I'll be taking notes for you." Tom felt sheepish reading the Bible in public. After Tod read a few verses, he asked Tom to read. While reading aloud Tom began to feel angry about the situation, about having been roped into a Bible study and now having to read aloud. After Tom finished reading, Tod summarized the verses for the group. Then one of the others read a few verses, followed by another summary from Tod.

During this study Tom felt patronized, talked down to. It turned out he was familiar with the verses they were reading and he didn't agree with Tod's interpretation. Tom found it peculiar that Tod was constantly stressing the physical pain Jesus endured after being sentenced to die. Tod graphically detailed how punishment was meted out in those times, with specifics about the implements used and the severity of the beatings. Tom hadn't remembered reading such things in the Bible before. Not wanting to have the study drag on, Tom kept his opinions and criticisms to himself. Tod seemed to be trying extremely hard to make Tom feel guilty about what happened to Jesus.

When the final verse was read, Tod asked Tom to talk about how the reading had changed him, if he would start praying every day, and what he felt. Tom replied that the readings didn't change him, that he doesn't pray and wouldn't start now; he said he had his beliefs, which were personal, and he certainly would not discuss them in front of strangers. With that said, he left.

The incident at the pizzeria had merely proved to Tom again that Tod's church was definitely not for him. For the next month he stayed away from Tod at work, but then decided to forget about it and not hold it against Tod anymore. He began speaking with him again, but the two had lunch together a lot less frequently than before the incident.

Recruitment

After a decade of friendship Tom and I were married in the fall of 1991 and moved to Brooklyn. Soon after the new year we hesitatingly accepted an invitation from the McKinleys to have dinner with Ronnie and Rita Tanner (Ronnie's an evangelist, and Rita a women's counselor with the Brooklyn Sector of the NYC Church of Christ).

To my surprise, the Tanners were only a few years older than I, and both had been accomplished performers before committing to the ministry. I realized later that the Tanners had been prepped by the McKinleys about Tom and me and our backgrounds, including our interests, religious affiliations, occupations, goals, openness to the church, and so on. (Later, I myself was taught by Rita to never go into a "situation" without a well-thought-out plan, which included knowing as much as possible about the person.) My ensuing relationship with the Tanners did not evolve spontaneously or with honesty. Our purpose was to make new friends in a new neighborhood, yet their goal was to recruit us into their church at any cost.

Days later, during a call from Joan, she mentioned that Rita led one-on-one Bible studies. This was followed by a call from Rita inviting Tom and me to the movies. I was happy to have made friends so quickly. Tom reluctantly agreed. The next week I began to study the Bible. It seemed so perfect. I was already attracted to learning more about my Christian faith and, I thought, "Who better to teach me than the wife of an evangelist?"

During this time I was bombarded with compliments for being "open." My self-esteem was boosted. Since my husband and I had different ideas about religion and had difficulty expressing them to each other, I didn't acknowledge his concerns as seriously as I should have.

The next three weeks were intense. Since my teaching job ended at noon each day, my Bible studies were scheduled every other day. Also, I attended weekly meetings with a small group of church members and visitors; these meetings were called Bible Talks. It was less informal than one-on-one studies. Bible Talks constituted an additional engagement each week. Soon I was told about Sunday and midweek services and was strongly encouraged to attend.

This schedule didn't allow me enough time to digest the material presented, or to develop genuine relationships. The lessons were not self-guided, as I expected, but instead were precisely structured with prepared questions, examples, and accompanying scriptures. (Not until I was baptized did I learn that members must complete a series of classes that formally instruct them in exactly how to teach these studies.)

I had thought of Rita simply as a friend helping me get started with the Bible, there to answer questions that came up; but, to my surprise, another woman led the first study. She, like me, was a shy, newly-married math teacher who had been raised Catholic. As time went on, other new faces from the church attended my studies. It was exciting to meet such seemingly sincere women who had a positive outlook on life. They appeared to be down-to-earth with respectable careers and strong families.

The church's agenda was intentionally kept from me. Baptism was the goal, although it was not discussed until "my faith was strong enough" to accept it. Baptism was reserved for the elite who demonstrated total commitment to the church's program, at least as much of the program as was presented to us at that time. (After baptism I was assured that I had only a small piece of the big picture and that the picture would continue to enlarge as I matured as a Christian.) Similarly, the International Churches of Christ's position that it was *the* only church of God was carefully fed to me bit by bit, as well as the church's interpretation of discipleship, confession, evangelism, and authority.

Information about me gathered by this network of "new" friends was reported to their leaders. (I know this because later I was taught to operate in the same way.) This allowed my studies to be custom tailored, to be emotional and very personal. During the studies the other women members would voluntarily share their life's experiences with me, their past fears and wrongdoings, dreams, spiritual struggles and victories. This created a supposedly safe environment in which I could be vulnerable. It also afforded them the opportunity to emphasize my weaknesses, and to use my desire to have a deep relationship with God to their advantage.

It was obvious to the others that Tom and I had a strong bond; getting to know me meant they also had to get to know Tom. From the beginning every effort was made by church members to befriend Tom, as artificial as it was. It irritated Tom, and it was uncomfortable for me, to have men from the church arduously force their friendship on him.

Since I spoke with at least one member each day, my leaders began to know Tom, or at least know about Tom, quite intimately: his likes and dislikes, hopes, fears, and especially his criticisms of the church. I sought advice from other women whose husbands were not members in order to help me convince Tom that his concerns were unfounded. I wanted Tom to be part of the excitement that I felt, to accept my new friends as his, and to develop an interest in the Bible. The more I pushed, the more he backed away. The more I became involved, the more I confided in my church friends, and the less Tom and I communicated.

All the members I met told a unique story of how God transformed them. Drugs, alcohol, and promiscuity were now in the past. I often said that it seemed too good to be true, but these doubts were quickly dispelled when others openly shared that they had had similar fears in the beginning.

Yet, I still had deeply buried reservations that surfaced the day I was scheduled to be baptized. I cried uncontrollably for hours and begged for God's assistance and courage. I was frightened of the commitment I was about to make. Other members had warned me that Satan would be working extra hard on me as I got close to baptism, so I was not surprised by my reaction. In addition, since they taught with extreme confidence and always had an answer that appeared to come from scripture, they had formed in me a solid foundation of submission.

By this time I believed that the church was an authority on the Bible and that I should not trust my own feelings, emotions, and opinions, or the opinions of those outside the church. The church had created an environment that I desired to be a part of, but I was not allowed to enter into it until I was completely willing to let go of whatever was keeping me from total submission. The church had determined that my "cost" was Tom and my family.

Out of desperation I called Joan McKinley to plead with her to help me. In a soft, loving tone she read a scripture to me about Satan roaming around like a roaring lion, implying that he was waiting to devour me. She encouraged me to be strong for both my sake and Tom's, and to not allow Satan to win another battle. Minutes later I dragged my feet to Rita's home and was baptized.

Tom had urged me to slow down, to not make a decision so quickly. He was leery about the church's methods of recruiting and proselytizing, as well as its extreme fundamentalist interpretations. He pleaded that at our infant stage of marriage, this would put theological differences between us like a wall of separation. Tom felt confused. He knew he didn't care to be a member of the church, yet he didn't think he had the right to tell me what my beliefs should be. He wanted to respect my beliefs. He was unnerved that I would be baptized into a different faith so soon after we had professed our vows in a Catholic service.

He asked me questions about the church's dogma, and we had many discussions and arguments about theology. He said that many of my theological reasons for believing so strongly in the church were not logically sound. He was also worried that a void would grow between us once I was baptized. He had seen the almost fanatical devotion of someone like Tod McKinley, so no wonder Tom worried that I might end up putting the same kind of energy and time into the church. He said that I would become a person different from the friend and wife he had just married. He was surprised to find out how much I, in fact, was committed to the church. In a sense Tom closely predicted our future. Needless to say, he was extremely upset when I told him I had been baptized in the church.

My aspirations when I was baptized were to be the best wife I could be, to have the best marriage, to be a better Christian, better daughter, sister, and friend in the name of God. Just the opposite occurred! Up until the second that I decided to break away from the church, I would have died for the NYC Church of Christ. I sincerely believed that God was leading the movement and that I was without question the happiest and luckiest woman to have been chosen for the "Kingdom of God." I worked very hard at imitating those whom I considered to be more "spiritual" than I. Because I genuinely demonstrated my commitment to the church, I was quickly being trained for leadership. Only months after being baptized I was co-leading a women's Bible Talk.

THE BOSTON MOVEMENT

Being in Leadership

Humility, commitment, and trust were some of the themes I was taught to focus on in the study meetings. These are admirable qualities in a person, but when they are redefined to suit only the church's ends, it becomes deceit. Never did I consciously suspect that I was manipulating others. I was sincere and wholehearted in my commitment, and unfortunately this is exactly what they used against me. My confessions, honesty, energy, beliefs, goals, and secrets were used to construct an unreal world in which I lived twenty-four hours a day. Shamefully and regrettably I did the same to others.

Being a member of the church was intense enough, but being a leader even topped that. After Sunday service a small group of leaders (called a Discipleship Group or D-Group), led by a higher leader, met to discuss "stats." Stats were simply the statistics for each Bible Talk, and included such information as which women were absent from services and why, did all my women give a contribution, how many visitors did my Bible Talk have this week, did I set up any new studies, and specifics on who could be baptized in the next couple of weeks. We then helped one another make a detailed plan for each of our visitors.

I recall the leader of my D-Group harshly rebuking us for taking too long in ordering *The Master Plan of Evangelism*. This book describes and encourages the use of deceptive conversion techniques (which I realized only recently)—for example, the author uses Bible verses to incorrectly advise withholding information from a new convert until the person is "ready" to have the grip of control loosened. I see this now as an illustration of the group's philosophy that the end justifies the means—that is, it's okay to manipulate because it's for a higher cause.

92

In D-Group I was given a two-page document, "What Leadership Is All About," which outlined practical suggestions to help organize my week. The document warned me that I would get less sleep and that it was imperative for me to be "vulnerable" (which meant be willing to seek advice and let all my thoughts be known to another leader). It was mandatory for me to discern who was on the "front burner." *Front burner* refers to a visitor who has been consistently studying the Bible with the group and attending Bible Talk and midweek and Sunday services. In other words, the person was "teachable" and had a good chance of being baptized within the next week or two.

It was also my responsibility to calculate which "sisters" (women from this church only) my visitors needed to meet in order to have "good talks" together. I determined this based on which sisters would influence a person the most. For example, if my visitor was a professional who worked Sundays and therefore had difficulty attending morning service, then I would introduce her to a "committed" sister who used to work Sundays before deciding that God comes ahead of her job. (Note the confusion in the last sentence: God is used as the reason for not working, but it is really to the NYC Church of Christ that one is making a commitment!)

The leadership document also stated that as a Bible Talk leader it was my duty to "fix" things so that there were new faces at Bible Talk. The buck stopped with me! If I or the women in my Bible Talk did not bring visitors to the services, then I was not considered spiritually well. Therefore, it was a priority for me to keep a watchful eye on my Bible Talk. I often wondered where God fit in.

It does not surprise me now that the only word underlined in that leadership document (besides the titles) was the word *contribution*. Another of my duties was to make sure that each woman in my Bible Talk gave her weekly contribution, and I was to know exactly how much. I was trained to have talks with women who were falling short in their tithing (which is set at 10 percent of a person's gross salary). I was taught to give women the following type of advice:

> • How is God going to "open the floodgates" for you (i.e., reward you) if you're not totally depending on Him?
> • How can you say you trust God if you don't trust Him with your finances?
> • Don't you want to be a part of helping to advance God's Kingdom?
> • It's not your money after all—it's God's! If the government can take money out of your paycheck, then why not God?
> • It will strengthen your faith in God and I know this is what you want.
> • You are being prideful and it is clear in the scriptures that God opposes the proud!

Early in my membership I recall being told that a friend of mine in the church (a member for at least ten years) had "fallen away from God" (left the church). This member had been a financial adviser to the Brooklyn congregation. She voluntarily helped budget families' finances so that they would be able to tithe. A year and a half later, after I had left the church, I was told by a friend of that woman that there was more to the story.

It seems that when she questioned the amount of money that the full-time leaders were contributing in comparison to other members, she was reprimanded and labeled as "divisive" by the church leadership. Leaders have their rent or mortgage paid for by the church and in addition receive a salary. She wanted to know why the members contributed 10 percent of their gross salary (from which they still had to pay their rent and living expenses), and the leaders contributed 10 percent of their church salary (from which they did not have to pay rent). Why the double standard?

Fear

Through scripture, I was manipulated into believing that if I were to leave the church, I would be leaving God and therefore suffer severe consequences. The church misrepresented Satan as being more powerful than God (although this was not explicitly said), which caused me to live in fear that my relationship with God could be pulled from under me without warning. After reading a scripture from Ephesians, for example, I was directed to ask myself: "Do I take seriously the scriptural teaching that there is an actual war going on and that my eternity is at stake?" and "Do I believe that Satan intends to do me as much harm as possible?"

Using quotes from Revelation they warned me that God would "spit me out of his mouth" if I was a "lukewarm" Christian. A lukewarm Christian was interpreted as a church member who didn't show absolute allegiance to the church's man-made rules (for example, someone who leadership felt did not smile enough or evangelize enough or confess enough or contribute enough). We were also taught that we would have been better off never having known the Truth than knowing it and turning our back on it. Church members took this to mean that there was nothing worse in God's eyes than to leave the church.

I began to fear what life would be like outside the church. In fact, I had a difficult time understanding how I had survived before I met the group. Thoughts, attitudes, opinions, and feelings that resembled myself before baptism were labeled as "worldly" and therefore were sinful. "World" was redefined to include anyone outside the church. I learned that the world was full of hate and evil, and that a "friend of the world becomes an enemy of God."

During a NYC leadership meeting, a guest speaker charismatically compared Satan to a lion stalking his prey. She described a typical kill in excruciating detail. She was careful not to forget to mention that a predator attacks the "weakest and least mature" of its prey. No member wanted to be tagged as weak but would rather be identified as a mature Christian; no member wanted to be devoured by Satan (i.e., leave the church).

I became blind to the obvious evils before me. My sister and her fourteen-year-old daughter were baptized into the church eight months after my baptism. A few months later my niece decided that she no longer wanted to be a part of the NYC Church of Christ, and it became my job (and my sister's) to warn her of the consequences that might befall her if she left the church. I was told by Joan McKinley to help my niece understand what she was choosing if she were to leave; I was to do this by describing in detail what it feels like to get burned on a stove, so that she would have a better idea of what it will be like in Hell. Joan also instructed me to tell my niece that without God she could wake up tomorrow with leukemia or get hit by a truck.

It was often preached that part of learning to be our best for God was to imitate those who were more spiritual, and that we should be grateful that God put these people in our lives. On many occasions Rita instructed me to speak softly and slowly like she did, to look into the eyes of the person with whom I was studying, to sit close to her, and, if appropriate, to gently touch her shoulder. (Rita, in turn, imitated women leaders who were higher in rank than she.) I viewed Rita's attention as an honor since it was obvious to me, and to others, that it was a rare privilege to spend so much time with a women's counselor. She challenged me to "attach myself to her hip" and to watch how she operated so that I too could learn how to lead effectively.

I learned how to respond in different situations, to recognize and advise women who were not doing "spiritually well," to speak with authority, and to be thorough and efficient at everything I did. Ultimately, this translated into my judging others as if I were Jesus himself, viewing anyone outside the church as not saved (why let God decide that?), deceiving and manipulating unsuspecting people, being totally submissive and obedient to leaders, and disassociating myself from my family and especially my husband.

My Marriage Suffers

My relationship with Tom quickly deteriorated. Before being baptized in the International Churches of Christ, a person must fully believe that only members of that church are going to Heaven. Thus, in my mind, Tom was on a fast train to Hell. What else was left for me to do but persuade him to follow in my path?

As much as I was trying to be all that Jesus preached, in reality I was quickly turning into the opposite. Communication between Tom and me ceased. I couldn't understand why he was rejecting the "new" Mary and saying that I was more Christian-like before I met the group. In my eyes I was striving to rid my character of such things as deceit, prejudices, and unkindness, when in fact without my realizing it I had become arrogant and manipulative.

Members of the NYC Church of Christ praised me for my courage and perseverance through this persecution at home. There was even a special support group called Women In Challenging Situations (for wives whose husbands weren't members of the church). I was led to believe that the more difficult the trial, the more faithful and spiritual I was before God. Beginning with the pre-baptism studies and later at the support group meetings, a connection was made between being godly and being persecuted, along with the notion that Christianity is neither safe nor predictable.

Many others consistently tried to convince me that my husband was dangerous and had uncontrollable problems with his temper, and that the difficulties we were having would have occurred whether or not I had gotten involved with the church. Tom's anger toward the church helped to confirm in my mind that he was indeed unknowingly controlled by Satan—since I believed everyone outside the group was—and that I was being "persecuted" just as the group said the Bible said I would be. The bottom line was that I desired to obey God, regardless of the consequences, and I thought I was obeying God by being part of the NYC Church of Christ.

During the year and eight months of my membership I moved out of my house to live with church friends on three occasions, the last time for a period of five months. From the first day of my involvement I was in a state of conflict and confusion. My world, which had consisted primarily of Tom and my family, didn't mix well with the church's manufactured world. A part of me would not accept the lies the church spread about Tom, and another part wanted to obey what I thought was God.

The day before I packed my bags for the final time was the day of my Heart to Heart talk. This is a scheduled one-on-one meeting with a leader, during which a person is asked a prepared set of questions. The goal is to weed out half-committed members. Such questions as "Do you have any unconfessed attitudes toward leadership?" were followed by a plan of repentance. I almost passed with flying colors! I was firmly advised that by remaining with my husband I was not trusting God with my situation and that I was in sin. Pure, selfless love meant "giving Tom back to God" in order to let God work on Tom's life. I had a very hard time accepting this. I wanted to give Tom the best chance to get to Heaven and to not do so would have been "selfish" of me. From the church's viewpoint Tom was obstructing my advancement into higher leadership.

Soon after I moved out my husband and family discovered through research and contact with my niece, who was now an ex-member of the church, that the NYC Church of Christ is considered by many to be a destructive organization, a cult. My husband's worst fears had been confirmed. Tom, my mom and dad, my other sister and her husband, and later my two brothers began to educate themselves on thought reform and the International Churches of Christ.

Being a teacher by profession, with no children of my own, I had the entire summer to devote to the church. My responsibilities tripled. My appointment book exploded with new names and phone numbers of people I was "reaching out to," luncheon appointments, Bible study dates, weekly one-on-one meetings with women from my Bible Talk, Sunday School preparations, Bible Talk presentations, baby-sitting appointments, and on and on. Every night during my separation from Tom, I went to bed physically and emotionally exhausted, only to wake up at 6:00 a.m. to pray and read my Bible before my first appointment. If no appointments were scheduled, I would create work in order to relieve the overwhelming feeling of guilt that I carried. There was no time to think about my husband, family, or friends outside the church. I recall wondering why I was incapable of shedding a tear over the loss of my husband. To ease my confusion, I thanked God for sparing me those painful emotions.

Only now am I beginning to understand that I was trained to reject any semblance of sentimentality. The church depicted Jesus as a man who struggled with his emotions, yet kept them suppressed, even while being brutally tortured. I strove to be like him. Pre-baptism studies focused on self-denial and not holding onto feelings and emotions. In fact, I was later taught to conclude a study by asking the other woman, "Are you ready to make the Bible your standard, instead of your feelings, opinions, religious experiences, traditions, emotions, or even what you see?"

Sermons taught me to be happy when persecuted and to smile when hurting. It was preached over and over that Satan uses emotions and "mistakes in my thoughts and reasoning" to drag me away from God and his church. After confessing to my women's counselor that I had had evil thoughts of leaving the church, she gave me a scripture to memorize. I was to recite "Take every thought captive" to myself every time I felt weak and doubted God.

A post-baptism study entitled "Dealing With Emotions" taught us that being "self-controlled" was to be without feeling. The study suggested reading Old Testament scriptures, substituting "my controlling emotions" for all references to "my enemies." Controlling emotions were any emotions that interfered with the church's control. Sadness was interpreted as ingratitude, fatigue as selfishness, defensiveness as pride, and criticalness as divisiveness. Thus, most instinctual emotions, feelings, and attitudes were considered sinful and therefore had to be confessed to the "appropriate person." The study I had been given concluded by suggesting that I meditate on the ways I had been "offering myself to obey my strong emotions" and to "think through the constructive actions that can replace my natural reactions." I see now that to kill and subvert a person's God-given emotions and natural feelings is unethical and dangerous to the human psyche, and is certainly not biblical.

Submit and Obey
As the months passed my ability to make decisions diminished to the point that I would literally beg others in the church to make decisions for me. I had no energy to think on my own. My innate logic and research skills were deadened. The church had created in me an unthinking, unfeeling machine.

From the first pre-baptism study to my last days in the church, as my dependence on the group increased, my decision-making skills sharply decreased. Soon after baptism a mandatory discipleship partner (DP) was assigned to me. This forced relationship required that I confess my thoughts and actions to my DP, submit to her authority, and seek counsel from her. Not even my worries were sacred anymore. We were also required to talk daily and meet weekly.

The more I was submissive and obeyed, the more I was rewarded with responsibilities, and the quicker I moved into a leadership position. The rewards were not without punishments, however. This system of rewards and punishments nurtured my dependence on the group, which made it difficult to be decisive. I was afraid to make a mistake since I no longer trusted my reasoning abilities; I was taught, and I noticed, that the consequences of a bad decision could be devastating.

After I proved to be of leadership caliber, I was given the women's counselor as my DP. Months later I was back to the original DP appointed to me after baptism. I held back tears and wondered what I had or had not done to be demoted. My self-esteem plummeted and I strove to be more "spiritual" than before. In addition, the neighborhood group that I was to meet with each week for Bible Talk was often changed, my living situation was shuffled a few times, and the Brooklyn church split into two churches when membership increased. It was also not uncommon at this time to see or hear of leaders at all levels having been fired from their positions. We were told only that God had exposed sin in their lives.

The church concentrated on scriptures that addressed childlike dependence, obedience, trust, and humility. Lessons emphasized being "vulnerable" and being "selfless" (putting others' needs, especially those of the church, ahead of one's own). *Pride* was a bad word used often among church members. Evidence of pride ranged from being late for service to missing a "quiet time" (daily, mandatory time reading the Bible and praying). A list of the symptoms of pride outlined in one study included not listening to the advice of church leaders, scorning instruction, airing your opinions, answering before listening, quarreling, and not confessing sins. I was told that I could not become "complete and mature in Christ if I resisted being personally counseled and corrected." Since the Bible was used by leaders whom I trusted, I believed that even though the advice was from another person, it was ultimately coming from God.

My leaders were careful to allow me to think that I could make autonomous decisions. They steered me into decisions without making it obvious by asking key questions, such as "What do you think God wants you to do?" and "How do you think Jesus would respond or act in your situation?" If I didn't answer satisfactorily, they would confidently say that God promised to make the best decision clear to me, and they would advise me to pray specifically about it. I was then directed to related scriptures for my personal study and reflection. Of course, God made it clear to me only when I did what the church leaders wanted me to do!

If I had already made a decision that they felt was unwise, then they would ask, "How can I help you if you don't let me know what you're thinking?" By being asked this question, I automatically believed that God was unhappy with the decision I made. I begged for God's forgiveness and promised God that I would try not to let Him down again. Significant decisions that I made that were strongly influenced by the church included whether or not to tithe, attend family celebrations, accept a job offer, vacation with my husband, separate from my husband, move back with my husband, divorce my husband, and so forth.

Other tactics were used to manipulate my decisions. They included character bashing in which I was accused of being wimpy, ungrateful, selfish, and, of course, prideful. To compound the tremendous guilt I felt, they would sternly remind me of the vow I had made at baptism to "make Jesus lord of my life," which included my decisions. As a follow-up, members who had been through an experience similar to mine would "encourage" me to be strong and want to spend time with me. Also, it was not uncommon to be mentioned anonymously in a sermon as an example of what not to do.

Unsuccessful Family Intervention

By the end of the summer my husband and family had hired an exit counselor. They wanted me out of the group, but they also wanted me to reason on my own that it was a destructive organization. When I realized that they wanted to present me with information on the church, I panicked and tried to flee.

Up to that point I had been consistently warned by leadership that I was a likely candidate for an exit counseling. The church had painted an evil picture of an exit counselor, labeling the information such a person would show me as "spiritual pornography." A half-year before I left the church, the church magazine cover story, entitled "Who's Brainwashing Who?," repeatedly described an exit counseling as an "agonizing and traumatic experience," one that leaves families torn apart. The magazine's cover pictured a frightened-looking man with tired bulging eyes and mouth open, sitting in a dark room watching a television screen that read: *Boston Church: CULT or Religion?* The word *cult* was four times the size of the other words. Faintly in the background, four men in dark suits hovered over the seated man, with one hand on his shoulder, preventing him from standing.

Although I knew that my family loved me dearly, I sincerely thought they had made a terrible mistake. I had been trained to not question the church's methods and dogma, so believing that my salvation was on the line, I firmly refused to allow the exit counselor to speak with me. Panic struck my family's faces when they realized how deep the control ran. They wept and begged me to listen, presenting me with the choice. I was not forced. But listening to this information was so difficult for me that when my family stepped outside, I surreptitiously phoned a church friend to let them know what was happening. Early the next morning three state police cars pulled up to the house. I stated my case to the officers and then left. As I drove away, I was emotionless and had no bad feelings toward my family. Even in that state of mind I knew that I would have done the same thing for my son or daughter.

Advice from the Group: Divorce and Legal Charges
The months that followed the unsuccessful intervention were hellish, although I was held with high honor by the church for having "escaped." I moved in with women leaders and was told to not give my family my address and phone number. I was strongly encouraged to not contact my husband and family for a very long time. (After one month I did call my mom and felt very guilty for having done so.) My leader's reasoning was to show my family that I should not be treated like a child.

Closely watched and pampered by leadership, I was told to write down everything that was said by my family during the attempted intervention, and any doubts or concerns that I may have had, so that I could deal with them biblically. To counteract my pain and confusion, I kept myself even busier. This was easy to do since I was rapidly promoted to lead a weekly Bible Talk of single women and women "in challenging situations." In addition, I was told to spend all my time with strong sisters and to go over the pre-baptism studies in order to strengthen myself.

It was during this time that the issue of my divorce was highlighted. Days after the attempted intervention, my women's counselor and many others said that it seemed as if God had made my situation with Tom clear and, ironically, that "*I* had to make some decisions quickly"—they were referring to my impending divorce. I was shown scripture after scripture on the subject, told to pray about the situation, and given phone numbers of divorce lawyers. After studying these scriptures over and over, I was not drawing the same conclusions. I would tell my leaders this, but they continued to encourage me to pray so that God would make it crystal clear.

I sensed that they were annoyed that I wasn't acting fast enough. My women's counselor even went to a higher leader who apparently knew Greek to confirm the meaning of *the* divorce scripture. Supposedly the scripture related to whether or not my husband was willing to live with me as a Christian. I was told that the leader said, with a laugh, that a husband is not willing to live with his wife if he tries to "deprogram" her.

Before the school year began I was accompanied to a New Jersey courthouse to file a formal complaint against my family. I was strongly persuaded to make a complaint, but deep in my heart I wanted no part of it. Fortunately, because I had said no when I had been asked by the state officer on the day of the intervention if I wanted to press changes against my parents, I now could not reverse that decision. The court clerk said that I was unable to file the complaint. I also made a trip to a Brooklyn courthouse to file for a restraining order against my husband. The process was much more complicated than my leaders had led me to believe, so I gladly gave up. I was extremely relieved since I wasn't doing this for me, but for my leaders simply out of intense pressure.

The Wall Crumbles

Those last two months seemed like an eternity. A few days before I decided to leave the church, all my pain, confusion, and guilt came to a head. Even though I was exhausted from fighting with my family and husband, frustrated that my family wouldn't back down on their position on the church until I heard both sides, and angered that my husband said he would contest a divorce, I missed all of them tremendously. I was disgusted that I was not allowed to call my husband and family or give them my new address. It deeply disturbed me to imagine my husband and family worrying about me and believing that I was involved with a dangerous organization.

Being so carefully watched and attended to by church friends also began to bother me. My DP practically carried me to the courthouse to file a kidnapping complaint against my family and to get the restraining order against my husband. This angered me; yet, for fear of being called ungrateful, I didn't let it show. I was beginning to not appreciate being manipulated into doing things I didn't believe in. My so-called friends were not concerned about my fragile emotional state, my intense confusion and loneliness, my inability to focus on my job, and my unnatural dependence on them, unless it in some way affected my continued membership in the church.

To discredit my family, church leaders told me that my family could not be trusted again and that my family did not respect my decision to be a Christian. I was told to allow God to work on my family members by "mourning the loss of them." In the church's attempt to slander Tom, the leaders predicted that during our separation he would have an affair, since all men have natural urges that need to be satisfied. I didn't accept that. In addition, I was frequently reminded that Tom and my family held me back from a truly deep relationship with God. God was making it easy for me to make a clean break, I was told.

I thought to myself that Hell could not be worse than the way I was feeling. For the first time I decided to do something against the opinion of the leadership. I begged my husband to take me to my parents' house for dinner. In my mind this decision could have equaled "falling away from God" (going to Hell). But I was willing to take the risk. Throughout this intense confusion I never forgot my family's cries that if I had the Truth, as I claimed, then it could withstand anything. What kind of God would abandon me so easily? I was so shaken that I couldn't drive. (I hadn't seen them since the unsuccessful exit counseling two months prior.)

Decisions About My Life

The visit was tense, but we were happy to see one another. That night I made another decision on my own to sleep at my parents' house. It was during lunch the next day that I asked my parents to find a person who knew the Bible well and had the facts straight. Part of me wanted to get my family off my back, and another part was vaguely beginning to see the danger of hearing only one side of an argument. I truly believed and was taught that the truth would prevail, no matter what the truth was.

The next day a woman who had been a leader in the Boston Church of Christ came to answer my questions and present the information I wanted to examine. That same day I confidently made the decision to break away from the group.

Initially, it was based solely on the realization that many of the church's teachings were not biblical. For the first time I read the New Testament in context and intensely studied the Greek and Hebrew translations of significant scriptures on confession, discipling relationships, authority, church structure, and bearing fruit. I had the opportunity to compare more accurate translations of the Bible to the one used in the church. It was obvious to me that I had been deceived. Up to that day I had accepted my leaders' interpretation of the Bible and never searched for the real meaning on my own. The exit counselor and I also discussed the published psychological studies of members of the Boston congregation of the International Churches of Christ. [Editors' note: see discussion of Flavil Yeakley's work in chapters 2 and 12.]

Everything began to fit together—although it was difficult to understand how deep the manipulation ran. How could I have been so blind? I was genuinely embarrassed, and genuinely thankful. Since that time I've never second-guessed my decision.

At first I desperately wanted to explain to my sister why I had made the decision to leave, but I also knew that my efforts would be futile since she was still committed to the group. I first needed to begin my own recovery process. Only after I voluntarily spent almost two weeks at Wellspring (a post-cult retreat center in Ohio) did I truly begin to grasp the underlying thought-reform techniques used on me by the leaders of the organization. I am now in counseling, and Tom and I are living together happily and also seeing a marriage counselor.

If friends from the group were to read this, they would not understand. They would consider it spiritual pornography and be angry at me for having written it. They would also feel sorry for me and would beg God to help me to come to my senses. Most members are sincere, as I was, about wanting to have an impact on the world; they truly believe they are doing so with God's stamp of approval. Someday, I hope, they too will have a story to tell.

It is still extremely difficult for me to sort out my experiences and emotions. A few months after I left, my sister Luanne broke away from the group on her own, although she no longer speaks with my family or me. I got my mind back, but not my sister. I love her dearly. My family is not complete without her and we desperately want her back.

I can honestly say that if it were not for God's mercy, and my husband Tom's unrelenting love for me, along with my family's undying love for me, I would probably still be a member of that destructive organization, which I now consider to be a cult.

Picture the most precious person in your life, and know that this group has the power to destroy even such a relationship. Do not underestimate the Boston Church of Christ.

9

Who Stole Your Freedom?[*]

Michael West

Thanks to Don
for being a true friend
and a great brother

Thanks to Jennifer
for helping me write this account
and for standing by me

And a very special thanks to
Steve Campbell, minister of West End Church of Christ,
I could not have done this without
your help, love, and encouragement.

I want it to be known that my motivation for writing this is based on love and concern. I have no personal vendetta against anyone in the Boston movement or against the movement itself. I love everyone in the movement. But I also

---

[*] Galatians 5:1.

want to warn those who may become curious about it. On the surface it appears that because of the Boston movement's tremendous growth, God is behind what the church is doing—and the members will be the first to tell you that. However, I do not believe that God is involved in something that is destroying the spiritual and psychological lives of His children.

At the time of this writing, I am a student at Vanderbilt University, where the Central Nashville Church of Christ (a "reconstruction" of the Boston Church of Christ) had been involved in so many policy violations at the school that all church representatives were asked to leave the campus and remain off university property. I was recruited by a campus minister assigned to Vanderbilt by the Boston movement and ended up being involved for about ten months. My involvement caused serious problems for me in school, at home, and after I left.

I began writing this about a month after I left the church. The first week I barely slept, and when I did I had dreams about the things that had happened during my involvement. During my waking hours I was constantly thinking about the things church members did, and I hurt so badly for those still involved because they are so deceived.

I had pushed out of my mind many of the things that had happened, yet memories constantly came up throughout the day. One reason for writing this was that I felt I had to do something to ease my mind. And I must admit that writing this has helped a lot.

Not being a psychologist or theologian, I will not go into the psychological or theological dangers of the movement. This is simply a record of what happened to me and things I observed that I believe are wrong or harmful.

112

Recruitment

I first got involved in the movement through David, a guy in one of my classes, who invited me to a Bible "discussion" that he led on campus. When I went I was surprised to see that he did not lead the study; someone named Kevin did. Afterward, everyone was invited to get together with the person he or she came with and study the Bible some more. When David asked me to study, I agreed.

This one-on-one Bible study, as they call it, is the beginning of a series of studies that teaches most of what the Boston movement believes. It was totally one-way, in that I sat and listened to a mini-sermon and answered a few questions while one person taught and another took notes.

After my first one(actually two)-on-one Bible study with David, Kevin (who was David's discipler) began to lead the studies. One study was known as the "Persecution study," in which John 15:20 and 2 Timothy 3:12 were read. The conclusion is that if you are persecuted, it means that Satan is trying to make you stop whatever you are doing. Therefore, whatever you are doing must be right. They do not teach that a church or individuals can bring persecution upon themselves.

Kevin then showed me some articles from the *Vanderbilt Hustler* (our school newspaper) about the controversy the movement was causing on campus. Part of the university's policy states that all meetings not held in a student's room or in a common place must be sponsored by a student organization and led by a student. The Bible studies on campus met neither of these criteria, which naturally caused many problems between the group and campus officials. Kevin had met with the heads of the school administration to try to work something out. The article quoted

Kevin as denying all connection with the Boston Church of Christ, saying that he was simply "trained" for the ministry in Boston. When I asked Kevin about this, he again denied connection with the Boston Church of Christ.

After several more one-on-one Bible studies, David and Kevin asked if I wanted to become a Christian, and I responded yes. They said that we must "count the costs," according to Luke 14:28–33. While counting the costs they ask some very personal questions. They go through Galatians 5:19–21 and ask which of the listed sins you have committed. They also ask if you are willing to give up everything for the sake of God's kingdom. This is when they determine whether or not you are ready to become a Christian, based on whether they are certain that you will submit totally to their authority.

Obviously, no one is told that this is how they determine if you are ready to become a Christian. The implications behind Luke 14:28–33 are whether or not you can finish the Christian life if you start it, not that you will submit in blind faith to another imperfect human! To be a Christian, according to the movement, you must be willing to do what the leaders say without question, which, for them, is the sign of "a true disciple's heart."

After these numerous Bible studies over a span of two months I was baptized into the movement on October 19, 1988. That very night Kevin told me that I must have someone in my life to disciple me so that I could grow to maturity in Christ and reach out to others and help them. Both of these sounded very positive so I did not question what he said. Besides, according to them, I was a "spiritual baby."

Someone named John invited me to dinner that night. We immediately became great friends, and I thought he would be discipling me. However, David was assigned to be my discipleship partner (DP). The term *discipleship partner* is a gross misnomer because partner implies equals. But, there is absolutely no equality in the discipling relationship.

At this point I had limited knowledge of the Bible and didn't know of I Corinthians 3:7, which says that only God can make someone grow spiritually, not the one who plants a seed, nor the one who waters it. The movement claims that you can grow only if you have someone in your life to disciple you, and that God helps someone grow only through other people. Many times it was said that God will not come to you personally, but through someone else. They sadly limit God's power.

Questions

About a week later someone left the movement. Everyone called her a "fall-away," so I naturally thought that she had left God. I called her, and she reluctantly agreed to have lunch with me. The first thing she asked was if someone from the church had told me to call her, and I told her no. When we met for lunch I quickly discovered that she had simply changed churches, not left God. So I naturally asked her why she was being called a fall-away. She replied that everyone in the movement thinks that the only Christians alive today are those in the Boston movement. She told me that she was going to a local Church of Christ that was not part of the discipling movement.

During our conversation she told me some things that I simply could not believe. First, she said that the Central Nashville Church of Christ was a "reconstruction" done by the Boston Church of Christ and that Kevin and most of the other leaders, including the lead evangelist and his family,

115

were directly connected with and financially supported by the Boston church. This of course made me question Kevin's honesty since earlier he had told me that he was not connected with the Boston Church of Christ.

Second, she warned me about the methods of discipleship they teach. Her father had recently died and she attended the funeral without getting permission from her discipler. Her discipler's discipler had made her sit down and read aloud every verse in the Bible about seeking advice. Only when she finally started crying did they allow her to go home. Her leaders said that she was "cut to the heart" about what she had done.

Third, she told me that she was a foster parent of a child in some third-world country to whom she sent about twenty dollars every month. She said that when her discipler's discipler found out about this, she was advised to stop sponsoring the child and instead give the money to the church. She was told that she should seek first the "Kingdom of God." The movement teaches that its church and only its church is the kingdom of God. They teach that doing anything that they are not doing or advising is not first seeking God's kingdom; therefore it is not pleasing God and not serving Him.

I was prepared to leave the church after this meeting with her. Since our conversation was longer than I had expected, I missed the very next "meeting of the body," which was a Wednesday night worship service. David asked me why I missed service, and I told him that it was because I had been talking to the girl who left the movement. I was then encouraged to tell David and Kevin everything she had told me so they could "take away any doubts I had." I told them I had planned to leave the church because of the things the girl had told me. For the next few hours, they convinced me that everything was all right, that the things she had told me were accurate but had been taken care of, and that she should not have left because she overreacted to everything. As I look back on this experience, I realize that they were already in control of what I did and the way I thought, after only a week's involvement on my part.

Getting Discipled

Soon after that David and I started having "DP times," during which he began to "help" me become more like Jesus. To quote from the lead evangelist at that time: "Discipleship is imagining someone like a block of stone, with Jesus on the inside, and chipping away everything that does not look like Jesus." David began to work on everything from how I spent my time (I had to spend more time on campus evangelizing) to the way I walked (sometimes when I walked I looked down, and David said that Christians should not look down).

At one time I had contemplated getting a doctoral degree in parapsychology. David told me I could not pursue it because it did not give God any glory. He said anything that did not give God glory was sinful. Well, David is a big fan of the rock group Rush (and I do not find anything wrong with their music at all). I told him Rush's music did not give God any glory, to which he never responded. I quickly found out that a disciplee can never point out something wrong in the life of a discipler who is "superior" or more "mature in Christ," or the disciplee will be labeled a bad disciple.

On November 4 and 5 the church's college ministry had a retreat, which I thought was great. Everyone had a wonderful, spiritually uplifting time. But the very next time the ministry was together, Kevin addressed us, saying that

117

during the retreat some people acted like non-Christians. I had no idea what he was talking about. Those students who Kevin thought behaved inappropriately were made to stand in front of the entire college ministry, confess what they had done, and apologize to everyone. I hadn't noticed anything wrong at the retreat, and even if someone had acted inappropriately, I would rather not have known about it. After everyone apologized, Kevin told us that since it was forgiven, we should forget. I wondered at that point why it had even been brought up.

I quickly learned from David that members of the church are expected to seek advice on a lot of things, most of which would be common sense. When I was in the movement, members were expected to seek advice on whether or not to renew their lease, where to live, whom and whom not to date and marry, when to marry (your discipler must decide if you are spiritually ready to get married), where to go and not to go on dates, and everything financial, including what to buy and what not to buy (one woman was told not to buy a certain car, but that she should buy a cheaper car and give the difference to the church).

David also said that the married people in the church are expected to tell their discipler about their sex lives so that their sex lives could be improved, claiming "you're discipled in every aspect of your life because it is God's plan." Once when my parents were at the lead evangelist's home, many people called to seek advice (ask permission) about whether or not they could stay home from church because their wives had the flu.

A couple of times when I had not sought advice about the slightest, most insignificant thing, I was made to feel as though I had sinned. Members are encouraged to make decisions based on their discipler's advice, not the members' faith. Yet Romans 14:23b says that "everything that does not come from faith is sin."

One day David gave me a sheet to fill out for a record of my membership. At the top of the sheet was written "Baptism/Re-baptism/Placed Membership" (most likely there is now a fall-away sheet filled out on me). I asked him what a re-baptism was. He explained to me that many times when people were baptized, they didn't know what they were doing, weren't ready for the commitment of Christianity, or didn't fully understand. When they "reach a higher level of under-standing," then they are truly baptized, and the previous time(s) are just "immersions in water." When they are re-baptized, their entire previous Christian life becomes invalid to them.

The movement claims that the "one baptism" in Ephesians 4:4–6 means that only one type of baptism existed when Ephesians was written (around 62 A.D.), which is the same baptism that exists today, as opposed to the three baptisms that exist in the New Testament: John's baptism of repentance, the baptism of the Holy Spirit in Acts 2 and 10, and the baptism in water for the forgiveness of sins. Since this is what they claim the one baptism means, they say the Bible puts no restriction on the number of baptisms (for the forgiveness of sins) a person may have. I know of some people in the movement who've been baptized five or six times.

Baptism in any other church was not considered a "valid" baptism by their definition. You must know and believe everything they say the Bible teaches about baptism, plus more. You must say the right things and have the right mind-set before baptism, and after baptism you must immedi-ately begin to evangelize and have someone in your life to disciple you, or it is not a valid baptism. It seems that they will do anything to make you believe you are not a Christian and to get you baptized into their church.

Whenever I disagreed about what they said the Bible said about something, I was shot down. In the very first two-on-one Bible study, they read 2 Peter 1:20–21 and determined from that verse that there is only one way to interpret the Bible. They leave the impression that the only interpretation of the Bible is the interpretation of the leaders of the Boston Church of Christ and everything else is a misinterpretation.

A good friend of mine who left soon after I did told me about a time when he asked a leader about a confusing subject. The leader told him the church's view and mentioned several Bible verses addressing the subject. When my friend showed the leader some verses contradicting what the church believed, the leader told him he was misinterpreting those verses. There are many cases where I think that the church has implemented something and then searched the Bible afterward for justification of their action or beliefs.

I really began to trust David (as was expected). Discipleship partners start out with a lot of flattery, until you are totally sure you can trust them. Then, they begin asking a lot of very personal questions, which are none of their business. They claim that it helps to talk about personal things so they can help you grow. But they say they "need to know the things you struggle with before they can help you."

When you get to the point that you trust your discipler and finally confess your sins to him or her, the discipler then goes and tells his or her discipler about the things you have confessed. They claim that it helps to solve the problem. Very often what I would tell David wound up reaching the ears of the congregation's lead evangelist, and who knows how many others as it traveled up the pyramid. They claimed that the leaders could help because they were said to have the solution to everything. Romans 12:2 commands us to be transformed by the renewing of our minds, not conforming to the ways of the world any longer. But in the group you were constantly told to recall sins you had committed so that you could confess them. Consequently, it's impossible to allow your mind to be renewed.

I told my discipler everything I did during the day and even about some of my private thoughts. In the beginning I tried to keep some things from them, but David began to ask me some very probing questions, which were designed to elicit this information. I became so entangled in the movement's teachings that when I sinned, I felt as though I had to get to someone to confess it before God would forgive me.

All of my time was taken up. Even when there was not something planned with the church, they often came up with something—for example, a meeting that everyone was required to attend. I lived with my parents, yet saw them only on the weekends (and the leaders even tried to get me to move out several times despite the fact I had no job). I had to rob myself of sleep just to get my schoolwork done. It got to the point where I thought getting a good night's sleep was sinful. My schedule was as follows: Monday, discipleship partner time; Tuesday, Bible study; Wednesday, house church; Friday, devotional; Saturday, whatever was planned with the college ministry; Sunday, church. And there were evangelism times, "friendship building" times, times to study the Bible two-on-one with people, and many other nonscheduled things. And I was not a leader! Leaders had to prepare lessons and studies, attend leadership meetings, and they had many other responsibilities. As college students, we could study or do homework only on Thursdays or late at night. Thus, those of us in the college ministry held many all-night study sessions.

David often missed classes because he overslept or was busy doing something with the church. One time I skipped one of my classes (before my involvement with the movement I had never skipped a class in college), and David found out. He told me that I shouldn't do that because I had to be a "good example to the non-Christians in the class." I then called David a hypocrite to his face because he missed classes often. He replied that a hypocrite is someone who says that he does something but in reality does not. Wrong, that's the definition of a liar. I soon realized that it was very common for disciplers to tell their disciplees to do something that the disciplers themselves were not doing.

Immediately upon joining I was encouraged to start dating, but only girls in the church (we could not even date girls from Churches of Christ not associated with the movement). When I was continually encouraged to date but still hadn't asked anyone out, David told someone to ask me for a date, which bothered me. We were required to have a date every weekend. One time when I didn't date for about three weeks, Kevin made me promise to have a date every weekend. For a college student with limited finances, this is very difficult. At one point I went out with the same person two weeks in a row, and I was quickly told the dating "rules." John, with whom I usually doubled, had warned me not to date the same person twice in a row, but I didn't listen. Some of the dating rules were only double dating, no dating the same person more than once a month, no more than two phone calls a week to the same person, only see someone on the one date a month or during meetings of the body.

More Questions

John and I had grown really close. Soon we could tell each other things and not feel awkward, as we did with our disciplers. It was a very healthy relationship. He went home over Thanksgiving break in 1988; when he came back, he said he was leaving the movement. This really hurt me a lot. I could understand why he had to get out because I felt the same frustrations and experienced the same betrayals as he had. Yet, I tried to get him to stay. He stayed in Nashville two more months to finish out the semester, and continued to live with Kevin during that time.

Kevin often said, "One characteristic of a cult is that you cannot leave on your own free will if you want to. So many people call us a cult, but they don't realize that you can leave our movement with no hassle." Wrong. Everyone (including myself) tried to persuade John to stay. I experienced the same trouble when I tried to leave about nine months later, because everyone kept trying to convince me that nothing was wrong.

My brother began to get involved in the church around Thanksgiving. After he ended his involvement, he and my father regularly told me of some terrible emotional abuses to which he was exposed while in the movement. Because I didn't experience the things my brother went through and because this is an account of my involvement with the movement, I will not include the things he told me. I mention it to show that what I went through was not an isolated incident, and that in my opinion everyone either directly or indirectly involved is damaged in some way.

THE BOSTON MOVEMENT

Because of my involvement in the church and the things my brother went through, my parents stepped into the picture. They saw numerous things wrong with the church but never put the church down in my presence. That's the wisest thing they could have done. If they had criticized the church, I would have considered it persecution and others in the movement would distort Luke 14:26 to rationalize, as I had seen them do with others. My parents simply told me the things they saw as wrong, and let me discover the church's antibiblical practices for myself.

I continually questioned various leaders about discipleship. I told them that they were making people who have no training become therapists and psychologists, and that some people have special needs that not everyone is equipped to handle. They showed me I Corinthians 10:13 and said that since we are all tempted with the same things, we are the same. Many times I heard them say that everyone—no matter how different in physical appearance—is basically the same: we have the same feelings, goals, and desires of the heart. And after a long involvement with the group, it becomes true.

I asked why we must confess everything to a noninvolved person (someone we had not sinned against), and they gave a list of scriptures: Proverbs 28:13, Matthew 3:6, Acts 19:18, Galatians 6:2, James 5:16, and I John 1:9. They also gave a list of scriptures to justify their definition of discipleship: Matthew 28:20, Acts 26:29, I Corinthians 4:16, 11:1, II Corinthians 8:12, Ephesians 5:21, Philippians 4:9, 3:17, I Thessalonians 1:6-7, 5:12-13, II Thessalonians 3:6-7, Titus 3:1, Hebrews 3:12, 6:12, 12:1, 13:7. If you read these scriptures, you can see many, many distortions.

When I asked David why he never confessed anything to me, he claimed that I could not help, that it was none of my business, or that he had already confessed everything to his discipler, Kevin. Often I heard, from many people, not just David, "I am the discipler, you are the disciplee, not the other way around"—essentially, "Do as I say, not as I do." Most disciplers put on airs that they are perfect, have no problems, and are not involved in sin. The fact is that they are not open, something for which they condemn their disciplees. Sometimes I heard David say that if he were to confess his sins to me, I would imitate his sinful self and not his Christ-like self.

The movement's main focus everywhere is on colleges and universities (for example, the membership sheets have a separate section for students). They claim that this is because students have a lot of energy, excitement, and free time to devote to evangelism and church activities, and that many students are very social and can reach a lot of people.

Whenever a member talked about moving to another city or transferring to another school, his or her only priority was the presence of a Boston-affiliated church. I often heard members say, when referring to another city, "There isn't a church there yet." It didn't matter if a city had more than 250 Churches of Christ outside the movement or any other churches; if there wasn't a Boston-affiliated church, in their opinion, there was no church there.

Once a church member went on vacation, which in itself is amazing because when you're on vacation, you can't invite anyone to your Bible Talk. While the person was on vacation, he drove over one and a half hours so he could be at a Boston-affiliated church, even though there were other churches close to where he was staying.

Christmas 1988 was on a Sunday. Some members of the church wouldn't go home to see their families because there was no Boston-based church in their area. They stayed in Nashville just so they could go to church. Many of my high school friends had come home during this vacation, and I naturally wanted to visit them. But when David and Kevin found out I was visiting people who were not in the church, they quickly said that my high school friends might tempt me to fall back into doing some of the things I did in high school. So they advised (told) me not to see these old friends, unless of course I invited them to Bible study or church.

I once asked why there were no membership directories. They told me that at one time directories were printed every year, and the mainline Churches of Christ somehow always got one. They then got in touch with the people who were no longer listed—the fall-aways. The Boston movement stopped printing directories so that the mainline Churches of Christ wouldn't be able to get in touch with the fall-aways. For some reason, they don't want those who leave the movement to go to a mainline Church of Christ.

I sensed that there was a spirit of competition to grow faster than other churches, particularly the mainline Churches of Christ, because the movement really thinks that if it doesn't reach the world soon, Christianity will die out and there will be no one left who is faithful to God. They always compared their growth to that of mainline Churches of Christ. And they teach some terrible untruths about those churches. We were taught, for example, that everyone in mainline Churches of Christ is dead spiritually, that no one got involved in evangelism, that there was no love within the members, and the churches would die out by the turn of the century.

At this point I had only been involved for about two months, but it was enough time for me to be indoctrinated by the movement. It was Christmas time, and I left the city to visit relatives. I could sense that the relationship between my family and me was a lot worse, even with relatives whom I saw only five or six times a year. All members of the movement slowly begin to replace their family with the other church members, which the church encourages. It is biblical to have close relationships with other members of a church, but not to substitute them for your family.

The last three days of 1988 John and I spent with Kevin and his family in Florida. During this time we saw a very different Kevin, and when we asked him what was wrong, he said that before we arrived there had been some family arguments. John and I could see that Kevin no longer felt the people he grew up with were his family, but now his family was made up of others in the church.

College Life: Recruit, Recruit

At a college ministry workshop in 1989 during the spring semester, the men and women were separated into different classes so that we could have a confessional time. We had to confess everything we did over the Christmas break. We were then told that we were going to "have a different approach at Vanderbilt" because there had been so many articles about the church in the school newspaper and in the *Nashville Banner*.

So, on the first day when students were moving into their dorms, we "stormed the campus," inviting everyone we saw to our first Bible Talk of the semester. When I questioned why we were going against the administration and showed Romans 13:1 to the church leaders, they in response showed me Acts 5:29, saying that we should evangelize as God wanted us to, and sometimes our Christianity causes us to not submit to the governing authorities. Unfortunately, I began to reject every authority except that of the leaders of the church.

Two significant things happened during this time. First, they abolished the dating rules. The lead evangelist said that too many women were leaving the movement because they weren't allowed to date outside the church. To prevent this from continuing, the church was making it easier to date.

Second, on January 8, 1989, Don, a brother who turned out to be my best friend since John left, was baptized.

Since it was a new semester, we all had performance standards that we were expected to meet. I was required to invite at least ten people a day to the weekly Bible study, and David asked me daily if I had met my "quota." Performance standards gradually got more and more involved and time consuming. The only time I ever heard the word *grace* was when they criticized other churches for being "too grace oriented and not focused enough on evangelism." They believed that making disciples was the only purpose of the church—I heard it said in sermons many times. All other things, like visiting the sick or helping the poor, were considered "playing church" and "not part of the Lord's will."

I began to defend the church at all costs, even though many times I knew that what they were doing was wrong, and afterward I felt bad. Whenever a classmate or friend would tell me something about the church, I would ask if she or he had ever been to a service, implying that everyone's fears and doubts were false rumors, but then everything appears normal if you attend a Sunday worship service. The main problems come once you're in the system.

The church focuses more on growth than on looking after members' problems and needs. Once I was told (not asked) to provide some things for a Friday night devotional, and I was told this with only four-days' notice. Little did they know (or care) that the same week I had three tests and a paper due. Despite the fact that I had no spare time, I tried my best to get things together for the devotional. Many times before when I had told them that I couldn't do something because of school, they would reply, "What is more important, your education or the Kingdom of God?" Obviously, if you respond with "My education," you will be rebuked. When Friday came and things were not prepared, I was later rebuked by David and Kevin. They had not asked or cared why things weren't ready. And I didn't dare tell them because if I had, I would have been rebuked for placing a higher priority on my education than on the "Kingdom of God."

I don't know if this lack of empathy is apparent throughout the movement, but I have heard some very sad stories about the obvious lack of concern the leaders have for the members. They always wanted us to bring in "influential" people so the church could reach a lot of new people through them. But they seemed to have little concern about the spiritual lives of these so-called influential people.

Another significant thing happened during this time: On February 1, 1989, Jennifer, my future fiancée, was baptized.

About that time we began to have Wednesday night house churches instead of the whole congregation meeting together. The Wednesday night house churches were separated into three classes: one for visitors, one for newer members, and one for older members. During this time Jennifer and I were in the newer members' class, an indoctrination class every member was required to go through and pass. This was frustrating because we were already college students with full workloads and this was one more class we had to study for, take tests in, and pass. When I asked why the nonmembers were separated from the members, I was told that the nonmembers should not hear what was being taught in the class for the members.

Jennifer and I began to date shortly after her baptism. One time we climbed a water tower to see the lights of the city. I told David about it, and he told me not to take her there again because "someone could have seen you and claimed that you two were doing something immoral up there." I laughed and told him that this particular place was nowhere near the city, and there was no possible way anyone could have known we were there. He replied, "Exactly! And if someone was there and saw you two, he could have said something bad about the church." It was as though he had not heard what I just said. Often I found it impossible to reason with David, so this occasion was not an uncommon occurrence.

David said, "Kevin wouldn't do something like that." He didn't say, "Jesus wouldn't do something like that" (which is questionable). I wondered why he wanted me to live up to Kevin's standards and I was really confused by this. Was he putting Kevin over Jesus? During the past six months I didn't think so, but now I began to wonder. Very often I heard David praise Kevin and say that he wanted to be just like him: "Kevin is a better Christian than I am"—contrary to II Corinthians 10:12. I never got to know Kevin all that well and was never impressed by him. Everyone always exalted Kevin, which disturbed me, because I didn't see very many praiseworthy things in him. One thing is for sure: I'm going to have to see Kevin walk on water before I say, "Kevin wouldn't do something like that" rather than "Jesus wouldn't do something like that."

All the members seemed to have an exaggerated concern for the church's image. In their opinion the church was "being persecuted" everywhere, for the sake of righteousness. So, the church had to be perfect in everyone's sight, conforming to the ideals of people and society rather than God. Everything about the church and in the church had to be perfect; there's no room for simple human error. So concerned were they with the group image that they would change anything and everything about someone if it was even slightly different from the norm. For example, Jeremy, a fellow student in the college ministry, had a nervous condition in which he flared his lips. Everyone has something that makes him or her different, and this was one of the traits that made Jeremy unique. David and Kevin told Jeremy that he must stop the habit because "it's distracting." That seemed ridiculous to me, but everyone had to portray the "perfect Christian image." This type of behavior was frustrating for me because, for the most part, I never cared what people thought about me; but the more involved I became with the movement, the more I worried about what people thought about me and the church.

Since I thought what David said about the water tower was silly, Jennifer and I climbed the water tower again (by this time we were dating on a regular basis). When David found out, he got really mad. He told me that what I had done was very sinful because I had directly disobeyed him. He then said that if we went up the tower again, Jennifer and I would be forced to break up and the old dating rules would be enforced on us. This sounded just like a dictatorship, and I made up my mind at this point that if things didn't change, I would leave the movement.

Jennifer and I started to grow closer to each other. I was disturbed by the fact that the group was beginning to dictate what Jennifer's and my relationship should be like. They read Jeremiah 17:9 and concluded that you cannot know the desires of your own heart because it is too deceitful. Therefore, you need someone in your life to help you understand your heart. Even in marriage relationships, contrary to what the Bible says about the husband leading spiritually, movement wives have discipleship partners to whom they must submit.

Life in the Group Continues

My parents were quite bothered that I was spending so little time at home. They went to the lead evangelist and told him. Only when the lead evangelist talked to Kevin and David about the situation did they change their minds and start allowing me to spend more time at home. Never did they admit that what they did was wrong.

The Vanderbilt ministry had been having all-night study sessions on campus; David encouraged me to start having them at my house so that I could spend time both with my parents and the ministry. One time when Jennifer needed to wash her clothes, I invited her and her discipler over to wash clothes and study. David jumped all over me, claiming that I was setting a bad example and setting the church up to be criticized. Yet this was the very thing he had encouraged me to do! All this happened right after David rebuked me for using Jennifer's computer to write a paper because I was "in a girl's dorm room with the door closed." He was afraid that someone might see us go in together and think that we were doing something immoral. This is just one of the many examples I could give of the paranoia in the church.

I was ready to leave again. I was tired of hearing that everyone not involved in the movement was not a Christian. I also was tired of hearing them limit God to themselves only and limit God's power to their version of discipleship. The sermons and lessons are a lot of hype and emotion, and that's all. And I really got tired of hearing the same thing every week in Bible study. They read Galatians 5:19–21 so much that everyone became desensitized to it.

When they read Galatians 5:19–21, they go through and begin to graphically expand on what is said. They list everything that is considered sexually immoral, including some things that many members had never even heard of before getting involved with the group. When I confronted them with Ephesians 5:12 ("For it is shameful even to mention what the disobedient do in secret"), they said that if we cannot talk about it, it cannot be confessed when the time comes (they *expect* us to fall into the sin), and that non-Christians need to know specifically what the passage means. The passage begins, "The acts of the sinful nature are obvious"—which in my opinion needs no explanation. This particular scripture is read often at Bible study, and it is impossible to allow your mind to be renewed (Romans 12:2) if you are constantly reminded of these things.

Even though I said I wanted to leave it was hard because everyone is so sincere and at times very loving. And since over time you've become isolated from those not in the movement, you soon have no friends outside the church. I had alienated all of my old friends who didn't get involved in the church. (When I finally did leave, I was a stranger at my own school and in the city in which I had lived for over fourteen years; I didn't know anyone. I am still trying to restore my old friendships.)

133

At the beginning of May 1989, our lead evangelist's son, Jake, came down from Boston and took over the college ministry. Jake soon became my discipler and we got along great. He's a loving guy. At this point I thought that things would get better. But Jake only discipled me for two weeks.

Questions Turn into Doubts

David's and Jennifer's disciplers were disturbed that Jennifer and I were spending so much time together, so David began to tell me things that Jennifer supposedly had said. When I confronted Jennifer, she had no idea what I was talking about. It infuriated me that they had so flagrantly lied, and to claim that Jennifer had said some of these things was un-Christian.

I went to David and asked why he had done it, and he claimed that Jennifer's discipler had told him everything and that I should work it out with her. When I went to her, she told me what she told David. What she told David and what David told me were not the same thing, and neither was the same as what Jennifer had really said. They justified their actions by saying that they were afraid I'd have a greater influence on Jennifer than her discipler would.

When exams were over, Jennifer went home to New Jersey for the summer. I really wanted to leave at this point, but I thought Jennifer liked the movement and I was afraid that she wouldn't leave if I did. Although we were about eight hundred miles apart, I thought that if I left the movement I'd be leaving Jennifer as well, since members aren't allowed to date anyone outside the movement. So I stayed. The summer was long and miserable, especially without Jennifer. Because of the time commitment demanded by the church I had to turn down some good jobs that I really needed.

All of my love, zeal, and compassion was being suppressed. When I first was baptized, I was going to volunteer for Campus Life, a Youth for Christ organization that focuses on helping high school students; it had helped me several times. I loved being involved with Campus Life; it was a great organization when I was in high school. Anyway, when David found out, he told me that I shouldn't volunteer, and that God didn't want me doing that since God wanted me to reach out to Vanderbilt students.

During the summer one of our evangelism "techniques" was to set up a volleyball net on campus. We didn't have to wait long before people joined us. Once I wanted to do this, and of course I had to get permission from my discipler, who told me it was not a good idea (ironically, he had done it several times and it had proven to be effective). Also, when people looked sad, I would naturally try to encourage them in some way. But many times they would reply that they would talk to their discipleship partner (DP) later. Help that did not come from their DP was not legitimate help; they believed that only their discipler could help them with their problems. These are just some examples of how the movement suppresses love, enthusiasm, and compassion.

A lot of changes happened over the summer, and I was not informed of any of them. For a church that pushes openness, it is the most closed about what happens. No one was ever told about people who left the movement until a long time after they left, if we were told at all. Most of the time you eventually notice that someone is missing whom you used to see every day.

Every time the church's version of discipleship is mentioned in a sermon, they follow by saying that it is God's plan for world evangelism. It seems to me that they are not totally convinced about it themselves and they have to keep telling themselves it is. I even heard in one sermon that if you are not being discipled, you are not going to heaven.

The college ministry was taught some rather unorthodox things over the summer. Previously, total obedience to a discipler had always been taught, even if that discipler is doing something wrong. They tell you "God has put that person over you as your discipler for some purpose, and we do not always know what that purpose is. He may be teaching humility and total submission to Himself." They began to teach that even if a discipler were a total idiot, his or her disciplee would still grow and become more like Jesus because "God would bless the disciplee's desire to become just like the discipler."

They taught that if you became a Christian out of fear of Hell or fear of God, it wouldn't last long for it would be out of the wrong motivation. In their opinion, becoming a Christian must be done out of love for God, never fear. And finally, to quote from one of the lessons: "God is a monomaniac; all he thinks about all day long is people becoming Christians. That is the way we need to be, only thinking about making Christians."

Very often, when someone outside the group questions the doctrine or practices of the group, that person is asked, "How many Christians did you make last year?" A question like that is designed to turn the criticism around onto the other person. Naturally, every Christian would wish they could have helped more people become Christians during the past year, but that shouldn't be their sole purpose. If you asked anyone in the movement, "How many brothers or sisters did you visit in the hospital last year?" or "How many poor people did you feed or clothe last year?," they would either be embarrassed; label you as unloving, unspiritual, or non-Christian; or state that that was not their purpose as a Christian. They use Philippians 2:5 in combination with Luke 19:19 to justify their singular focus.

After being in the movement for some time I read Flavil Yeakley's *The Discipling Dilemma*. My eyes were really opened to what was going on in the movement. Much of what he describes existed in the church. I knew now that I had to get out, but I had to talk to Jennifer. (It was now the end of the summer of 1989, almost ten months after I had joined the group).

Reinforcement and Decision

During the summer, relations between Jennifer and her family were terrible. By the end of the summer, she was more than ready to come back to Nashville, so I went up to New Jersey and accompanied her back. On the way back to Nashville we talked. I was so relieved to find out that she wanted to leave the church as well, but the only thing that had stopped her was fear of losing me. Knowing that she wanted to leave also gave me the courage to go. It is much easier to leave the movement with someone else; it provides mutual support.

The night I tried to leave, Jeremy asked me to tell him what was wrong with the movement. As I was explaining, Kevin came up to us. I told Kevin some of the things that I knew were wrong with the movement. Immediately, he began to rationalize and offer excuses. I told him that what the church defines as discipleship was wrong, to which he replied, "Everyone is being discipled, either to become more like Jesus or less like Jesus."

I asked him where it said that in the Bible, but he never answered me. I asked him, "Does that mean that for over 1950 years, before discipleship as you define it was practiced, everyone became less like Jesus? And what about the sincere people in the world who are doing great things but are not in the movement? Are they not growing? Are they not going to Heaven?"

His only reply was, "Well, if they are becoming more like Jesus, they must have someone in their lives to help them."

Kevin agreed with some of my statements and told me that I should stay and change the things that were wrong. Previously, when I had tried to stay and change small things, nothing ever happened. Therefore, I knew that nothing would change if I stayed now and tried to change things. I felt as though I had no choice but to leave.

Kevin then told me that my reason for leaving was not discipleship or any of the other doctrinal errors I had brought up, but it was because I was holding a grudge against someone. He quoted Matthew 5:23–24 and said that I should stay and "be reconciled to my brother." I honestly didn't hold anything against anyone in the movement, and I still don't. It took me over two and a half hours to break away from Kevin and Jeremy that night, and even then, I had to promise to get back in touch with them. If I hadn't told them that I had to get home, I would've been debating with them all night.

About a week after Jennifer and I left the movement, I received a phone call from Don (with whom I'd grown close). I could tell in his voice that he had to get out as well. It was a lot harder for him to leave since he was a leader. Don experienced some of the same things I did. Since his involvement in the movement, he had lost all of his friends outside the church. Because I had left, it was easier for him to leave. He also had been planning to leave but couldn't do it alone.

It says something about the movement when a twenty-five-year-old can become so fearful that he has to pack up, sneak out of his own apartment, and leave town when no one is there to question him.

On October 7, 1989, Jennifer and I went to Jeremy's wedding. Naturally I wanted to talk to everyone I hadn't seen in so long because of my love for them, but everyone in the college ministry, even David, avoided us. Only two people talked to me at any length: Jeremy and Peter, whom I hardly knew. I don't know for sure but I suspect that the others were told something about us. Members avoided us so much that I actually thought they were afraid of us. One person asked me where I was going to church, and I told him I was going to a local mainline Church of Christ and that the people there were great. At this, he started to laugh, which really hurt. He said that he'd been to that particular church, but as far as I know, he's never been to any mainline Church of Christ. That attitude toward mainline Churches of Christ is indicative of the closed-mindedness of people in the movement.

Looking Back

While I was in the group I had risked losing my scholarships because my grades dropped substantially. Afterward I found a night job and began to do better in school than when I was in the movement and didn't have a job.

I realize that the reader may think the movement is horrible and that all of my experiences were unpleasant. I'm sorry if that's the case. I had many great experiences in the movement that I'll never forget. And if I've made certain people sound unloving or uncaring, I'm also sorry. There were many times when everything and everybody were wonderful, but also times when the leaders acted inexcusably. The bad times far outweigh the good times, and even if they didn't, the other dangers of the movement make it necessary to avoid it.

I want to reiterate that I hold nothing against anyone in the movement. For the most part, everyone involved appears to be very sincere in their service of Jesus and therefore they do not realize what they are doing. The group introduced me to my Lord Jesus Christ and for that I will be eternally grateful. What I've recorded here was written out of that love.

To all my friends whom I may have hurt while I was involved with the movement, I'm sorry. I was wrong. Please forgive me.

To the reader who may be excited about the growth of the church or the reader who is studying the Bible with someone from the movement, I implore you not to get involved. It may appear totally innocent on the surface, but deep within the system, emotional and spiritual lives are being destroyed. Some of my best friends have left Christianity altogether because they received a false view of it from the movement.

To the reader who is in the movement, I want you to know that this is not persecution for righteousness's sake. I used to think that everything against the movement was. But I have seen and experienced a lot (and certainly nowhere near everything) of what happens in the movement and I knew it was wrong and had to get out. Please read James 3:1-2, Ephesians 4:11-12, I Corinthians 1:10-15, 7:23, Galatians 2:4, 3:25. Also know that what you believe or are being taught about traditional or mainline Churches of Christ is not true. I have not been to every Church of Christ, but the ones I have been to are great. The members are just as (if not more)

140

loving and committed as the members in the Boston movement, despite what you may have heard.

To the reader who may have been involved in the movement and in leaving has left God as well, I encourage you to give mainstream churches a chance, despite what you have heard and been taught by the movement. You will be surprised, just as I was. I did not leave the movement so that I would stop being a disciple of Christ. I left so that I could start.

To the reader with loved ones involved in the movement, remember that the person involved will stay in only so long as the movement seems to fulfill some need (while in fact exploiting that person's faith). I knew for a long time that the movement was dangerous and wrong, but I didn't leave until I was sure that the need I had would still be fulfilled outside the movement. So please find the need that is keeping them involved and fulfill it. I urge you *not* to attack the church in their presence or forbid them to be involved. Doing this will almost ensure that they will run and cling to the church even more, thinking that you are persecuting them. The church will then tell them that Luke 14:26 says that they should hate everyone that hinders their service of Jesus. So if you do this, you will push them further away. Showing anger is about the worst thing you can do. Instead, you must love them more than ever.

You must also respect them, something that many people with someone in the movement do not do. Don't create untruths about the movement or assume that it's doing what other unorthodox groups are doing. The members know what does and does not happen (for the most part) and if you tell them something you're not sure about and it turns out to be false, this may drive them away and make you look ridiculous. For example, when Jennifer was in New Jersey over the summer, she heard from someone that there are mass weddings in Boston. That's the craziest thing I've ever heard about the movement and it's simply not true.

Also remember that one characteristic of thought reform is that the subject doesn't realize that it's happening. So, don't tell them that they're "brainwashed" or again you will push them away. Members of the movement are victims; the last thing they need is further victimization from their families.

10

The Hard Way: How I Came to My Understanding of the Difference Between Religion and Cults

Shalon Goldsby

Remembering my childhood is not easy. Most memories of my growing up come back to me in daydreams, at most a blurry reflection of those events which brought me to my existence and beliefs today. Yet, one thing I do remember vividly is the look of sadness and concern on my father's face when I told him for the first of many times that I did not share the same Baptist beliefs as he did. His forehead wrinkled and his sad brown eyes glanced over me in pity as he shook his head and predicted, "Well then, you will have to learn the *hard way*."

Almost five years later my father's words still haunt me, mostly because they have proven to be true in every facet of my life: in relationships with people, in excelling in school, in overcoming occupational obstacles, and especially in choosing a religion. It is almost every parent's dream that their children carry on family traditions, yet when children choose not to live up to those aspirations, much bitterness and confusion is likely to ensue. My parents blamed themselves when I deviated from their religious orientation, and in doing so, missed their opportunity to question my new "religion." In retrospect, I do not believe that I chose a religion. A self-proclaimed "religion" chose me.

To give you some background, I'm in my fourth year at the University of California at Berkeley. From the second half of my freshman year, April 15, 1993, until March 23, 1994, I belonged to the San Francisco Church of Christ (SFCC), a western affiliate of the Boston Church of Christ (BCC). This chapter includes how I was met, my first impressions of the group, the mind-numbing and humiliating Bible studies I endured, my indoctrination into the group, an overview of my involvement, and my final assessment of my total experience in relation to the group, which I now consider to be a cult. For all practical purposes, I have replaced actual names with pseudonyms. Italicized words are those used frequently within the SFCC to promote solidarity among its members, but also may help to distinguish this group from legitimate Christian organizations.

Personal Background
I grew up in a nonreligious environment in the sense that my family rarely went to church, hardly ever prayed before a meal or going to bed, and seldom cracked open a Bible. Just the same, I was considered to be a Baptist all my life. Both my parents were raised in very strict religious environments, both brought up by single, black Baptist women. Both my parents, for their own reasons, turned away from the ritual of religion, and sought their own ambitions, though still praising God

144

from time to time. My only guess is that these are echoes from their childhood.

While strict religion was put aside, economic ambition was strongly emphasized in my family. Growing up poor and black, my parents sought the American dream in nice houses, big lawns, fancy cars. In order to achieve their material dreams, my parents had to and continue to work very hard. Unfortunately, our home life suffered as a result.

Forced to attend a predominantly white high school where I was often the only black girl on campus, I was very alienated and lonely. My parents thought that the only way for me to achieve economic success later in life was to attend this particular high school. When I tried to talk to my parents about how miserable I was in being such an obvious minority, they merely shrugged it off and told me they were tired from working so hard so that I didn't have to grow up in poverty like they did. When I got accepted to UC Berkeley, my parents were very happy for me because this marked another step in their legacy of economic success. I was very happy, too, because I would be attending a multicultural, interracial school for the first time in many years.

Coming to Berkeley, I was very unprepared for the reaction I would get from such a multicultural institution. Many white students asked me questions about my blackness that were just as ignorant as the ones asked by the white students at home. Many of the black students spurned me because I did not come from the ghetto and I had led a "privileged life." For the first few months I mostly hung around students from Asian or Latino backgrounds, yet still felt alienated when they began to speak their other tongue or relate to one another through their cultural similarities. I often questioned my own existence around them, as they did not make very much eye contact with me. Only as an after-thought did they invite me to their parties or to eat in the dining commons with them, and once again, I found myself all alone.

First Contact with the Group

In February 1992 I was eating brunch in the dining commons in the dormitory where I lived. I got up to put away my tray and as I stood in line waiting for the conveyor belt, I noticed a mixed girl with a gigantic smile, excited eyes, and curly hair jumping up and down saying, "And he is so *awesome*! And we're going on another *date* this weekend!" She seemed overly excited, but I paid it no attention.

After I had placed my tray on the belt, I turned around and found myself face to face with her. She looked at me with a tenderness that suggested that I was her long-lost sister and said, "Hi! My name is Janice. Would you like to play volley-ball with me and some friends of mine?"

"No, thank you," I replied. "I don't know how to play." I started to walk away, but she blocked my path once again.

"Oh, well, that's okay. Neither do we. We're just learning how. *C'mon*. It should be a lot of fun."

I agreed, and that next Saturday I was out playing volleyball. The girl who had invited me was not there. She was on her date, so I just played with a friend from the dorm whom I had invited to join me in my humiliation. I was having fun, until I noticed that something was very strange. Two men whom I didn't know were hooting and hollering for me on the sidelines. Every time I fumbled and missed the ball, the guys on my team hissed at me, while the men on the sidelines cheered me on: "C'mon, Shalon! *You can do it!*" Whenever I hit the ball correctly, the men on my team just appeared to be relieved, while the men on the sidelines shouted overexcitedly: *"All right,* Shalon! *You go, girl!"* I found out later that these two strange men were Janice's friends, and that the men playing on the volleyball team were just ordinary students living in the dorms.

That night I got a phone call from Janice inviting me to come and check out her church. I said sure. I had nothing else to do, so I went.

First Impressions

Multiculturalism and Cultural Tolerance
The service was in a hotel ballroom in Concord, a neighboring community that's a good forty-minute drive from where I go to college. When I asked Janice why the service was so far away, she said they moved around frequently because their physical bodies were their places of worship.

When we walked in, I was impressed with how gentlemanly the men acted. They didn't leer at or flirt with the women, and they referred to all of the female members as their *sisters.* Unlike some of the black Baptist churches I had sporadically attended during my life, this religious group encouraged multiculturalism. Blacks, Latinos, Chinese, East Indians, Native Americans, Japanese, whites, and others gathered together under the same roof for one sole purpose—*to worship God.*

As Janice led me down the aisle to our seats, we were greeted by just about everyone. "You actually know all of these people?" I said.

"Yeah," she answered, looking dreamily into the distance. "We take care of one another."

147

THE BOSTON MOVEMENT

Opening Singing

The service began when four older men (two blacks, one Asian, one white) called *song leaders* took the stage. The crowd cheered the *head song leader* on as he led us into a very upbeat and lively song, which all the members knew by heart. Janice arranged for me to have a songbook and passed it to me, squeezing my knee in overly enthusiastic glee.

Confession

After the song, a married couple came to the podium. The members of the audience continued to cheer on. Both discussed how *sinful and immoral* they were before they *came to God;* both described how and when they were *met,* motioning to the member in the crowd who recruited them, at which point the crowd's attention shifted in admiration of the *fruitful disciple.* After telling of their *baptism* and subsequent *forgiveness,* both members reiterated the *power of the Cross (Jesus' death)* to work in our lives.

Communion

After *confession* came *communion,* the traditional passing of the bread and wine. I wondered why such a modernized group would stick to such an old custom, but I didn't question it for the bread and grape juice were coming around, and since I had not eaten since the night before I was hungry.

When communion came to me, I broke off a huge piece of bread and stuffed it in my mouth, then washed it down with the thimbleful of juice provided. It was tasty.

Janice looked at me in shock. I found out later that communion was a *spiritual* event that only members were allowed to take part in it.

The Message
Suddenly a hush fell over the crowd of bowed heads. A short, dimpled white man with a big smile took the podium alone. The crowd erupted and cheered with the tenacity of a nation welcoming its new king to the throne. "C'mon Michael!" "*You go, bro*'" "All right now, Michael!" Michael was the *lead evangelist for the sector*.

Michael proceeded with his message ("C'mon, Michael!"), which began by informing the crowd of the depraved state of *the world* ("*Yes*, Michael!") and the *immorality* of all mankind. He went on to describe how God had great plans for us ("Yes, Lord!") before *we went astray and threw it all away with our sinful ways*. He then told us to *hear the message, read the Bible, repent of our many sins, get baptized, help make more disciples* ("You go, bro'") and *keep going to God daily*. He reminded us that *we must remember God, or else, God may not remember us*.

After reading some very guilt-inducing (*convicting*) interpretations of scriptures from the Bible, Michael told us that we were all special and loved by God. He urged *disciples* to *study the Bible out* with *visitors*, and for visitors to *open their hearts to the Word of God*. ("Amen!")

Parting Songs and Fellowshipping
The song leaders took the stage again, and we sang three more songs before the service was dismissed. During this song, members and visitors stood, linked arms, and held hands to show their *unity* and *love* for one another. I had never seen anything like it in my life—certainly at none of the black Baptist churches I had attended.

After the service Janice introduced me to some other members before we went to lunch. All were very interested in me, asking how I liked the service, then about my family and background. Later Janice called me on the phone and asked me if I would like to *study the Bible*. I said sure.

Bible Studies
Bible studies were given to prospective new recruits in varied order depending on the needs of the recruit. The studies I went through were *The Word, Discipleship, Baptism, The Kingdom, The Cross, Light and Darkness*, and *Counting the Costs*. Each subsequent study was supposed to narrow my options more and more, until I *broke* and begged them to *save my soul*.

The following is a synopsis of these studies and the ways in which they were administered. Blinded by the promise of being *saved*, I endured the verbal abuse of the studies. Also, the group advertised itself as fun, caring, and safe, making sure they met my needs, served me.

The Word
My first study was an introductory one in which Janice asked me personal questions about my *relationship with God* and whether or not I felt I was *serving God with my whole heart*. After she persuaded me that I was not *serving God* by just going to school and doing well, she showed me a scripture in Jeremiah about how God "has plans" for me to "prosper."

The study consisted of a cycle of verbally abusing (*rebuking*) me for my *past sins against God*, then praising me for my desire to be *right before God*. I was scared, but very much relieved at the same time.

Discipleship
A week later Janice brought Paula, a fellow sister, to the Bible study. Paula took notes while Janice threw obscure scriptures

at me from the Bible, asking me to interpret them. I would give my opinion of what they meant, then she would rebut my responses, reading the scripture again and again until her version seemed the only valid one.

Janice kept drilling Matthew 28:19 into my head. It was supposedly *"the last command."* The cult referred to it as the *"great mission."* The scripture—and even a year later I know it by heart—says:

> Therefore, go, and make disciples of all nations, baptizing them in the name of the Father and of the Son and of the Holy Spirit, teaching them to obey everything I have commanded you. And surely I am with you always, to the very end of the age.

And this, I was told, is how *a true Christian or a disciple of Jesus* must live. *"Christian equals disciple equals saved,"* reminded Janice.

Janice, Paula, and I sat, read, interpreted, reread, and reinterpreted scriptures until I was convinced that I was not saved.

Baptism
A few days later Janice, Paula, and I *studied out baptism*. Janice and Paula made a big deal about the practice of *baptism* and how those of other churches were invalid. SFCC of the BCC required *full immersion* of a new disciple into a body of water. Showing me several scriptures where the saved were immersed in water, Janice and Paula reiterated the importance and urgency of becoming a disciple. In all of the scriptures, they showed how the people who immediately heard the *Word of*

God practically went diving into the waters of baptism. The urgency served to speed up the process of my recruitment into their system.

The Kingdom

The most confusing and ill-taught study for me was the *Kingdom study*. Surprisingly, this study led by the *women's counselor* (female assistant and wife of the *lead evangelist*) consisted of a barrage of prophetic scriptures from the Old Testament and apocalyptic scriptures from Revelation. The women's counselor, Monica, seemed confused even when she tried to describe the metaphorical meaning behind the signs and visions of the past and future.

The study did not last as long as the other ones, and I began having more doubts. Afterwards Janice and Monica talked to me enthusiastically about school and my family, soothing me. They made it seem as though every word from my mouth was the most intelligent and insightful thing they had ever heard. Later, while walking me home, Janice asked me to bring *a list of my sins* to the next study.

The Cross

A few days later Janice and I *studied the Cross*. Janice took me to a small, private ice cream parlor where she insisted on buying me a cone. After having chosen a table, Janice reached into her backpack and pulled out what appeared to be a report.

"Did you bring your *sin list*?"

"Yes." I gave her the list of feelings of anger and hatred toward my family, the frustrations I had with my college social life, and the resentfulness I had for being alienated throughout high school.

"Okay." She glanced over the list, to my horror. It was something very private. Between me and God.

Janice handed me a booklet. "Now read this."

I read the title emblazoned across the front: *A Medical Analysis of the Crucifixion of Jesus Christ.* The report was lengthy, detailed, and highly graphic. Supposedly, a doctor had analyzed the *crucifixion of Jesus* and had come up with some startling conclusions. Apparently, as the report stated, *Jesus did not die on the Cross, but after having been bled on the cross for long hours and then finished off, a large rod shoved up into His intestines by dissenters.* I was extremely disturbed by this piece of literature.

"So what do you think?" Janice asked, noticing the discomfort in my face.

"It's pretty gruesome." I really didn't know what to say.

"Yeah, and to think, *you did it to Him.*"

"What?!"

"*You killed Jesus, just like they did. Just look at your many sins.*" She ran her fingers over the list. "*With these sins, you have nailed Jesus to the Cross! But everything is going to be all right. God will forgive you. You must become a disciple.*"

I was far too confused to ask any more questions, and certainly too stupefied to object. I looked at the medical analysis one more time, reading about the horrible *death of Jesus Christ.* I began crying out of fear.

"*You feel guilty, I know, but it's all right. God will forgive you. You must be baptized.*"

"Can I take this home and think it over?" I motioned to the report.

"No," she quickly grabbed the report and shoved it into her backpack. "This is my only copy. *The Bible should be all you need to make your decision.*"

I wondered why she chose to show me that supplementary report if the Bible was all that I needed in order to understand why I should become a disciple. But by then I was afraid to ask questions. I was afraid of how I would look before them and their God. And I was very much afraid of *going to Hell.*

Light and Darkness

I had been studying the Bible for a month when I did the *Light and Darkness study* with Janice and another sister. This study would make or break me. I was persuaded to believe that I had to be a disciple if I was to ever get *into Heaven.* So I was hooked, even though I did not agree with some of the interpretations of *sin in Light and Darkness,* such as the one that said that *my looking at a guy whom I considered to be physically attractive was the same sin as killing forty people on a subway.*

I was told to look at *spiritual* and not *worldly* aspects of things. Janice reminded me that I was to forevermore associate with *God's kingdom* and to *refuse the world.* Dating outside the group was forbidden. Friendships formed with people under any other premise than to recruit them were frowned upon. We were the *light* and everyone else was lost, in the *darkness.*

Warnings

My friends warned me. A few friends in the dorms showed me a BCC dating guidelines information packet. I did not believe that the BCC and the SFCC were affiliated. I laughed when I read the packet, as it was outdated and written from the perspective of more conservative Easterners. They even showed me a teen magazine article about a girl who left one of the so-called International Churches of Christ and how her life had been permanently altered. Relatives of former members called me and told me what I was getting into. Even my father said, "Why are you doing this to me?" when I told him that I no longer wanted to be considered a Baptist, but a disciple. "Dad, I am not doing this to you. I am doing this for you."

Counting the Costs

I was baptized on April 15, 1993. Before the baptism, I did the last study of becoming a disciple, *Counting the Costs*, which consists of *confessing any last-minute sins, and then dedicating yourself to applying the Bible to your life, making Jesus your Lord.*

I brought along the magazine article written by the teenage girl. I had decided beforehand that if this group had anything to do with the same group that girl belonged to, I would have nothing further to do with them. The girl had left the group because of the tremendous pressure the cult put on her to be perfect, or at least to live up to a standard of perfection. I told Monica to read the article and please tell me if I was about to join the same group mentioned in that article.

Monica glanced momentarily at the article, then set the magazine face up on the table. She whipped out her Bible and plopped it down next to the magazine and said, "Which one are you going to listen to?"

As I looked down at the teen magazine, I saw a naive cover girl on the front page with a big, stupid grin. The headline said something like, "How To Have the Boy of Your Dreams Wrapped Around Your Finger." Below that in fluorescent ink it said, "I Belonged to a Cult!", then something about prom nightmares. I looked at the Bible and it looked back at me with seriousness. I chose the Bible. Monica and Janice were elated.

Post-baptism

After I was baptized, disciples I did not know came up to me, hugged me, asked me how I was doing. But I had a hard time being out of myself. I was never a socialite, and getting dunked and *forgiven for my many sins* did not change a thing, as I thought it would. I had to eventually force myself to converse with others during *fellowship*; yet most of the time, I spoke of worldly things like parents, school, friends, jobs, grades. I rarely spoke of spiritual things like *my relationship with God, how much I loved God, or what I was willing to do to serve God or the leader.*

Janice became my *discipler* (spiritual boss). She and other disciples constantly verbally abused me over what I talked about when I talked to people. I was not deep enough, and in order for me to be deeper and more spiritual, I had to be *closer to God*. I *prayed, fasted*, skipped classes, avoided friends who did not go to the cult; I completely cut myself off from all things not connected with the cult in the name of *carrying out God's purpose*.

Growing Spiritually Older

During the next few months I noticed many changes in my life. Janice, once eager to hang out with me and be a friend, focused all her attention on recruiting others. Frequently, I knew I had a lot to say to people, but I could not for fear of getting verbally abused (rebuked) in return. All feelings of doubt were stifled, and I cried almost every day. I thought that my crying was a sign that I had come closer to God, when actually, we were further apart than ever. I couldn't even trust my own judgment when it came to reading the Bible. All my thoughts and actions were exposed and changed to fit the cult's interpretation of the Bible.

There were many events in particular that really opened my mind to the hypocrisy, deceitfulness, and cruelty of the group. These major events caused me to eventually withdraw (or in the group's words, *fall away*) from the SFCC of the BCC.

1. Once, in *fellowship, a brother* asked me what I prayed for when I prayed to God. I told him, even though I felt very uncomfortable answering such a personal question, that I thanked God for the disciples, my biological family, and other things, like for beautiful days.

The brother got extremely upset and said firmly in front of a large crowd of people, *"You better be praying for Jesus and thankful that He died on the cross for you!"*

I was extremely confused, hurt, and angry after this unprovoked confrontation. I tried to talk to several leaders about this brother's behavior toward me, but they all brushed it off saying that I was being *too emotional, and that I was in sin.*

Months later the same brother approached me again at another service. He had remembered me. *"Sister! What do you pray for now?!"*

I lied and told him that I *imagined Jesus' blood as He died on the Cross for us.*

The brother praised me. I had never before felt such shame and confusion as I had felt at that moment.

2. Once I was at child care, which is when members are chosen to come into service early and have an early miniature service because they must take care of people's young children during the regular service.

We sang a song before communion. The song was all about *Jesus dying on the Cross, and his blood covering our sin, and how we were so evil to do such a thing to Him, and how we must be continually broken over our sins.* It was a song meant, I thought, to provoke deep thought and self-analysis, a serious song. The song leader demanded that we smile in joy while we sang this slow, melancholy dirge. I did so, because I was instructed to by a *more spiritually mature,* male member. I was so confused and angry when the song was over that I wanted to cry. I felt like someone had whipped me, telling me that he would not stop until I laughed from the joy I was receiving.

3. Over the summer, some precult (worldly) friends and I had planned a trip to Mexico, for which I had worked to earn the money. The cult was really against vacations. They even urged college students who lived out-of-state to stay in Berkeley over breaks, so that they *could serve the ministry and not be tempted to digress to their old ways.* Well, they let me go to Mexico because I had already paid for the trip and I did not appear to be *struggling spiritually.*

While I was in Mexico, I had a great time away from the disciples, despite the fact I supposedly indulged in *sexual immorality.* I had some sexual thoughts about some men on the beach and was sexually attracted and aroused as a result. In addition, I had watched a very provocative movie in the hotel room I shared with my high school friend. I had to confess all of this and more to Janice when I got home.

"Did you think about Jesus at all while you were in Mexico?"

"What?!" I was shocked and upset that Janice would ask such a question.

"Jesus died because of people like you—sinful people who compromise! He died because you were sexually immoral! You nailed Jesus to the Cross, again! You're a murderer!"

After she forced me to give a moment-to-moment description of every last *sinful* detail of my trip to Mexico, I was reduced to shame. I felt so guilty for the week after my return home that I was ashamed to show my face. As time passed, my discipler forgot about what she had said to me about Mexico. I never did.

4. At an *all-campus devotional* we were read a scripture about faith, and the *evangelist* distorted it to mean that we were all *sinners* and that unless we started bringing more prospective recruits in, God was going cut off all connections with us. I felt attacked and humiliated. Later I told a sister how awful it was for the evangelist to get up on the pulpit, squeeze that scripture dry, and call us all sinners just because we were not *growing in numbers* as rapidly as he had wanted.

The sister said that she did not feel attacked, but *inspired.* She gave me a funny look, as if I was being ungrateful and should have enjoyed the verbal abuse.

5. We were commanded to perpetually think of ways to invite people to services (*share our faith daily*). At first, inviting one person a day to service was enough. After a while, demands increased. The cult demanded that we make a lifestyle out of recruiting new members. One inspired brother set a week's goal of inviting one hundred people, speaking to more

strangers than I speak to in a year. There was no longer such a thing as free time. All time was spent doing things for the *advancement of the Kingdom.*

If we did not bring people to services regularly, we were branded as *ineffective* and *sinful (struggling)*. As with many elitist "religious" groups, the SFCC of the BCC believes that all who do not belong to their group are going to the fiery *depths of Hell,* although they may not mention this to a new recruit, only after weeks of subtle persuasion or months after his or her indoctrination. My life became a mad struggle to save my family, my friends, and the entire population of the world.

6. We were told that everything we have, we do not deserve. *All we had was given to us by God for the benefit of the Kingdom.* Women sold their diamond wedding rings; men sold their sport cars. They did this in order to be able to give special contributions.

All this is under the guise of *saving the world.* Once or twice a year we were forced to fork over fifteen to sixteen times our regular *weekly contribution (10 percent of our weekly income)* for *special missions contributions,* the betterment of much-talked-about-but-never-seen overseas establishments. Since it's very difficult to obtain 153 percent of one's income, we often had fund-raisers. One middle-class man would not do this, saying the Bible claimed that he must hand over only a tenth of his income. They *disfellowshipped* him for *dissent.* Likewise, I was warned that if I were to lower my weekly contributions for any reason, I would be in serious trouble with the cult's *financial coordinators* because of my *irresponsibility.* I washed cars, worked overtime, and even took out an emergency student loan to help pay for my second special missions contribution.

160

7. Attendance was mandatory. Everyone was urged repeatedly and strongly to bring a friend to services. I went on *prayer walks* in the freezing rain and cold when I had flu, to *mid-week services* when I had yet-to-be-written, ten-page papers due the following morning, and to *campus devotionals* when I would rather have gone to the movies like all the other college students on Friday nights. When I wanted to go to a comedy club with some precult friends of mine after a campus devotional one Friday, I was verbally abused (rebuked) for not discussing my activities with my discipler first, for being *independent*.

8. Commitment was mandatory also. Sunday service: 5 hours; Monday Bible Talk meetings: 2 hours; Tuesday Discipleship (confession) times: 2 hours; Midweek service: 5 hours; Friday campus devotionals: 5 hours; Saturday dates: 4 to 5 hours.

If I had a paper or a report or a lab or a problem set due, I had to schedule it around the group activities. If I was tired because I had stayed up all night to finish homework after group activities sucked up all of my time, I was branded as *sinful for being undisciplined*. It was a perpetual cycle.

9. I had a class with a gorgeous man who did not belong to the SFCC of the BCC. He kept looking at me from across the classroom. I looked his way once and had to pretend that I was disgusted by the attention he was giving me. During the rest of class I kept sneaking peeks. Later that week I was talking to a sister when I mentioned him nonchalantly.

"Oh, by the way, I sort of had some *interest* in a guy outside of *the church*."

"When?!" Her eyes were becoming frantic and worried.

161

"Earlier this week." I said, not noticing her growing anger.

"Why are you telling me just now?!" It became obvious she was becoming unglued.

"Because I didn't think it was important. I didn't look at him with interest but once, and after that only to pretty much give him the idea that I was not interested." I sensed a rebuking, so I fumbled to correct myself to no avail.

"*It's still sin to be attracted to someone outside of the church. And it's an even bigger sin now that you've let it simmer!*"

"But nothing happened!"

"*Satan works! The next time he sees you, he might ask you to get together to study at his place. You go over there, 'like an ox going to slaughter.' You're attracted to him. One thing leads to another, and before you know it, you're in serious sin!!*"

I was being rebuked for things I didn't do, but things the *leaders* imagined I would do because they didn't trust my judgment, and they certainly didn't want me to trust my own.

10. I remember that for several months each night before I went to bed I would pray on my knees that God would kill me overnight so that I did not have to go on another day as a disciple. I found life unbearable and alienating. All that mattered to me was going to Heaven. I realized that I didn't care whom I hurt, how much money I wasted; all I wanted was to get to Heaven. Even when I prayed these things out loud in circles with my *Bible Talk and Discipleship Group,* they "Yes Lord"ed and "Amen"ed my death wish prayers to God.

The Turning Point

I think the turning point occurred when I was really burnt out one night because, with the group's activities and my obses-

162

sion to do well in school, I had slept only four hours in a three-day span. I was so exhausted on Friday that I could hardly keep my eyelids peeled open. I was hanging out with my discipler and her other disciple at a cafe. Both were older than I spiritually and, therefore, my leaders. We were going to *confess our sins* to one another and then go to the campus devotional.

"Shalon, you're being awfully quiet."

"What? Oh yeah, I'm just tired. That's all. I only got about four hours of sleep in the last three days, and I'm not all here now. I can barely process what you say, much less respond to it."

"Oh, well, that works for you, but think about us! I mean, we're tired too. It's *very selfish* of you to sit up there and not at least *try to be out of yourself*."

"But I'm tired."

"Jesus was tired."

For some reason, at that point in time, I knew more than ever that I was not Jesus and that I never would be. I knew it, but I knew that I couldn't say it for fear of rebuke.

"I can't even think." Which was true. I was not going to lie anymore.

"Well, *obviously, you're in sin. You refuse to live up to Jesus' standard!*"

I started crying and babbling, but my words were as incoherent as the thoughts that formed them. The other sister turned to me, smiled, and laughed out loud at my tears.

"Ya know, I think that these feelings you're feeling are *just feelings*." They both laughed and so did I, a quiet, con-trolled, pacifying laugh. When they saw that I had lightened up, they carried on with their conversation. I was silent again. "What was wrong with having feelings?" I thought.

Realization

I left the cult on March 23, 1994. I finally came to terms with the fact that the cult had torn me away from my family, shattered the majority of my friendships, crushed my dreams of becoming a writer, an educator, or anything for that matter, and hurled me into a bitter and confused relationship with God. Most of all, though, I knew that the lie I was living was never going to get me into Heaven. I did not think that I was or ever would be forgiven for *my multitude of sins*.

I decided to leave after reading a scripture in Psalms. It was Spring Break and I was up early one morning having my *quiet time*, my required morning prayer, Bible reading and application. As I read the scripture, it became more and more clear to me that I just did not understand what the scripture was trying to say to me. In a reflex, I reached for the phone to call one of the disciples for an interpretation. Then, with the receiver in midair, I thought, "Why did I have to ask them? And what difference did it make anyway?" I was only getting up early, pretending to be *close to God*, and essentially ruining my life to be accepted into their group. That was the moment when I decided to leave the SFCC of the BCC.

I finally called the Cult Awareness Network hot line in Chicago, a number I found at the end of the teen magazine article which I had kept throughout my cult involvement. I decided to research more on cults and why the SFCC of the BCC fitted into this category.

One leader informed me that although I had said I had wanted to commit physical suicide while in the group, *in leaving I was committing the more heinous crime of spiritual suicide*. I cut off my communication with the members after that chat. Since then Janice called me several times to tell me that I was *selfish and lacking in integrity* for not wanting to talk to her. In

164

the same breath she said that she *loved me* and that she *wanted to show me the Way.* She was intermittently abusive and caring.

Total Assessment

The Passing of Time and Knowing God
As time goes by, it is easier to understand the manipulative tactics the cult used to suppress my own beliefs and to distort the Bible for their own use. Reading about coercive groups in general as well as specifically about the so-called International Churches of Christ has not only helped me to identify the psychological dynamics that keep such destructive groups intact, but has also deepened my understanding of my own social and cultural weaknesses and strengths.

One recurring problem I have is setting apart the cult's interpretation of God and my own. I have convinced myself that even if He sends an angel to me telling me to go back to the cult, I would rather burn in Hell than heed that angel's warning. Yet, I have come to understand that, unlike the cult's *love*, God's love is unconditional, and he has plans for me, "plans to prosper." I really believe in that with all my heart. Exit counseling and therapy have helped me to realize that. Also, researching different cults, including my own, has helped me to see the differences between religion and cults.

Back into the Mainstream
People's reactions within the cult to my leaving were predictable, but I was entirely unprepared for the reactions I got from those outside the cult. Because of these reactions, I have decided that there is a great deal of ignorance in my community when it comes to understanding the cult mind-set.

One guy who left the cult because of his desire to "fornicate" kept calling me to remind me that *Satan had a strong hold on me* as well, alternately telling me to *repent of my sins* and inviting me to join him in his *spiritual depravity*. One soul seeker who wasn't in the cult reminded me that unless I began to immediately attend other churches and find God elsewhere, that indeed I would have committed spiritual suicide.

Having also been in contact with other student former cult members, I have discovered that even though they have left the group, many still think and act with the cult mind-set and will have nothing to do with cult awareness, believing that it does not concern them.

The Positivity in a Negative Experience

I think that God strategically placed this situation with the cult in my life to teach me a valuable lesson: that I must trust my own judgment and no one else's. If my lesson with the cult had not occurred, I would still be getting used by people, letting so-called friends trample all over me. Now, I am my own self, and I try very hard not to worry about people's perceptions of me, to see myself as deserving of great things in life, and to love myself unconditionally.

All of this may sound self-centered and egotistical, but I do think that the most difficult thing in the world is to love others when you cannot even love yourself. A lot of people in this world love themselves so much that they forget to love other people. People in cults think that they are loving the world by denying themselves the right to love themselves. I have found, through my experiences, a happy medium.

What I have learned is that everyone must decide for herself or himself what lifestyle, what religion to follow. Right

166

now, I see life as too complex to narrow my choices down to just one religion. Even though many people have suggested that I have "lost my religion," I do not believe this was ever the case. How could I ever have lost *my* religion? I may have lost my parents' religion, or the cult's interpretation of religion, but I have yet to completely lose *my own religion, the way that I choose to live my life.* Indeed, I have learned about religion the hard way, but when you think about it, is there really an easy way to learn anything?

Why I Am Involved in Cult Awareness

Last summer I went to my first meeting of a local support group for former cult members. I strive to make the issue of cults on campus more widely known in my local area. In addition, I hope to make materials defining and identifying cults more readily available to those who may need them before making life-sacrificing decisions. Such cult awareness resources and support groups are needed on campuses and in communities everywhere, especially in populous campuses and regions where students and others become numbers on a list and specks in a cold, impersonal crowd of thousands.

11

The Stranger in My House: A Parent's Story

Kimberly Logan*

I never imagined that one day I would be faced with having a child in a cult. I thought those groups were only for weirdos who made a conscious choice to be part of something apart from normal society. It was something that other people did and it had nothing to do with me—until June 1992 when my daughter joined the International Churches of Christ (formerly called the Boston Church of Christ).

Karen was bright, beautiful, and talented. I didn't know it at the time, but that is exactly the type of person cults are looking for.

Karen's career goal since she was fourteen was to pursue opera or classical music, either on stage or teaching. In her senior year of high school, Karen was awarded three scholarships to study voice performance at one of the best music schools in the country. By the age of nineteen, with her college choir, she had performed on stage with Pavarotti.

---

* All the names in this chapter are pseudonyms, including the author's.

Lincoln Center, Carnegie Hall, the New York and Philadelphia Philharmonic Orchestras were part of her college experience. It seemed that Karen had a promising career and a happy life ahead of her. Family, friends, and music were the nucleus around which her world revolved.

Recruitment

All this hope for the future began to change with the entrance of the International Churches of Christ into her life. The summer she returned home after completing her sophomore year at college was when they first began recruiting her. But even before she was affiliated with the group, I knew a change had taken place that made her almost like a stranger from day one of her arrival home.

The new Karen was the result of her involvement in one or two small Bible study groups on campus. Suddenly, she seemed to have an insatiable thirst for the Word of God. It was an obsession that caused her to frantically search for a Bible study for college students, even to the point of thumbing through the yellow pages of the telephone book searching for a church that had beliefs in alignment with her own.

When the International Churches of Christ came into Karen's life, she thought it was the answer to her prayers. The leaders of this group convinced her that God had specially chosen her to be part of this church.

It all started when Karen was waiting tables at a trendy restaurant and the wife of the evangelist and their little girl happened to be two of her customers. Their casual encounter resulted in an invitation to Karen to visit their church.

In fact, Dianne, the evangelist's wife, called Karen at home to make sure she would not miss the special midweek service. Two church leaders from the New York church would be the guest speakers.

Karen went and the next day she told me she had been "blown away" by the words of Joan Baker, the evangelist from New York. Her eyes danced with excitement as she talked about the fascinating lady and her great ministry to God in New York City. I had never seen my daughter so mesmerized by one person.

On the following Saturday, Dianne was back at the restaurant with a group of young ladies all about the same age as Karen. She was very much impressed with their friendliness and jumped at the chance to join them for a cookout that night.

There Karen met more friendly faces and warm smiles. Dianne was the honored guest, and Karen had the opportunity to learn more about her ministry with the church. When Karen announced she had to leave early, the church members urged her to stay longer. She told them she had promised a friend she would go to a local nightclub to see him perform in a band. In a subtle way they tried to get her to change her mind, hinting that a club was no place for a Christian lady to be. Despite their urging, Karen left and promised to see them in the morning at the Sunday service.

There was a dilemma, though. My husband and son had gone camping and left Karen and me with one car to share. I wanted to go to my church, but I knew Karen was dead set on visiting this new church. The solution was for me to go with Karen.

"Mom, you will love this church! The members are the nicest people I have ever met in my life!"

She was right. From the looks of the group, any parent would have wanted their child to associate with such a nice, friendly, polite group of young people. They showered us with attention and asked lots of questions, as though they genuinely cared about us.

The service was held in the ballroom of a downtown hotel and the place was "jamming" with hand clapping to songs and enthusiastic remarks interjected during the evangelist's sermon. Accustomed to the quiet reverence of a Methodist service, I thought this environment must just be typical of a charismatic church. Never did it occur to me that this church was part of one of the fastest growing cults in America. On our way back to the car I commented that I felt the members had treated us as though we were non-Christians, and Karen agreed that she had the same feeling.

I think it was her effort to set the record straight about her spiritually that made her agree to meet a young woman named Ashley that Sunday afternoon for a "one-on-one" Bible study. I urged Karen not to go, because she was to visit her grandmother who had not seen her since her arrival home from college. However, Ashley had been so persistent that Karen felt obligated to drive across town to meet with her.

Somehow this person was able to convince my daughter that she was not a Christian at all and did not understand the true teachings of the Bible. She said Karen had been misled and misinformed all these years by mainline religion which was full of falsehoods.

Karen was persuaded to attend an urgent Bible study that took place every day, usually late at night after she had been on her feet all day waiting tables. If Karen had to work at night, then she would go to Ashley's home after work and spend the night.

Personality Changes

Karen was outraged when I said her new friends reminded me of Moonies and it seemed like the church was a cult. As we continued to argue day after day, Karen said there was "spiritual warfare" going on in our household and that Satan was using her parents to try to keep her out of the church.

A few nights after the Bible study started, Karen seemed upset about something; when I asked her what was wrong, I was shocked by her response.

"I just found out today that if I were killed in an accident, I would go to hell because I have not been baptized into the Church of Christ," she said sadly, avoiding my gaze.

It was enough to spin me into action. The next morning I made some phone calls to find out about this group. I still remember the words of a pastor from a mainline Church of Christ, which is not associated with the International Churches of Christ in any way: "I'm sorry I have to tell you this, but your daughter is in a religious cult."

When I called the Cult Awareness Network in Chicago, they said they had more complaints about this group than any other. I met with a pastor from another Church of Christ and he gave me a stack of material on the International Churches of Christ. As I read the information, my heart sank.

All the articles and books discussed two practices of this church that are not found in the mainline Church of Christ. The International Churches of Christ has a discipling ministry in which each church member is assigned a discipler who gives advice on all matters to the person under him. This discipler has total authority over the church member and must be obeyed completely. The harmful effect is that the person becomes totally dependent on his or her discipler for all decisions.

Another concept practiced in this group is imitation. This means that the church member must imitate his or her discipler in every way. This causes complete loss of identity and autonomy. For example, an introverted person may be forced to become an extrovert even if it does not come naturally to him or her.

With Karen's recruitment came "the invasion of the body snatchers" or, more accurately, the invasion of the mind snatchers! It seemed that our home was bombarded with church members. Sometimes I would come home from work to find them sitting around in our family room. The phone would ring from early in the morning until late at night, always church members anxious to speak with Karen.

Within a very short time my husband and I noticed changes in Karen. She was like a zombie, not sleeping enough, not eating properly, and taking no time to care for her appearance. In fact, she started looking more like Ashley, very natural and casual, not at all like the young woman we knew who could easily pass for a glamorous model. We started to worry about her pale, haggard appearance.

Another source of worry was the sudden change in her when she spoke of her religious beliefs. Her voice would become monotone and her eyes would glaze over. It seemed as though we were conversing with a robot that had been programmed to say certain things.

One of the worst times for the family was attending Karen's baptism into this church, which took place only two weeks after her initial contact with the group. My husband and I confronted the evangelist and his wife and told them we hoped they would back off now that the "urgent" Bible study was over. Karen said she was so embarrassed by our rude remarks, but I thought we displayed as much composure as possible considering the rage we felt.

Over the next few weeks Karen spent all of her spare time with the group either at a church function or a social event. Every Saturday night there was a different guy coming to pick up our daughter. She was not allowed to date outside the church and only allowed to double date. No hand holding or kissing was permitted. Karen told us that dating is different in "The Kingdom."

As Karen attempted to recruit her friends into the group, I stayed one step ahead of her, warning them that she was in a cult and urging them to stick by her through the ordeal.

To our horror, we found what is known as a "sin list"; at the top of Karen's list was music. She was told by the group that music was a sin in her life because she put it before God. They even told her it was idolatry. It was bad enough that they were trying to take her away from us as much as possible, but now they were taking her away from her first love—music. Karen no longer rehearsed her voice at the piano, as had once been her daily routine.

Attempted Exit Counseling

We were desperate to do something to get Karen out of the group. We began to make calls to exit counselors. Exit counseling is a process much like deprogramming, only it's a voluntary decision by the cult member to engage in the discussions. The cult member must agree to sit down with the exit counselor and others on the intervention team (usually former members) and go over information about the group that she or he hasn't been allowed to see. Also discussed is

174

thought reform and how it is used by the group. The process of exit counseling usually takes three to five days.

We decided to try an exit counseling with Karen during our vacation away from home, when we were all going to the beach. On a Monday morning in July we brought in an exit counselor and a former member of the International Churches of Christ to begin the process of showing Karen what the group was really about. After the first morning session we took a break. Without our knowledge, Karen went to the nearest phone booth and called a church leader. Within hours the leader and two young church members appeared on the scene.

Because of their interference, the intervention was not successful. Back home, Karen was treated like a hero by church members because she had survived the "terrible, demonic" ordeal. Karen felt we had betrayed her, and it took several months to regain her trust. Total trust has never been restored and never will be as long as she remains part of this group.

Transferred About

In the fall Karen went back to school and became a member of the New York Church of Christ. She was assigned a new discipler who controlled her thoughts, actions, and every aspect of her life. We sensed that her transition into this church did not go smoothly and she appeared to have doubts. While Karen was at home for Thanksgiving, it appeared that the group here picked up on her doubts. I could only assume by her renewed commitment that she had been reindoctrinated and the movement's thinking and attitudes were reinforced.

Somehow Karen managed to keep up her schoolwork in spite of the time demanded by the group. Her visits home at Christmas and spring break were spent catching up on sleep she had missed and spending time with church members here. I'm sure Karen felt like she was the center of a tug of war, being pulled in different directions. Everyone was demanding her time—her school, her family, and the church.

It was better that Karen was hundreds of miles away because with her at home it was a constant reminder to us that she was part of a destructive group. While she was at school we didn't have the steady flow of phone calls or her constant rushing off to be with the group. We had a break from it, but still it was on my mind. I couldn't stop myself from thinking about the continual emotional abuse and the pressures on my daughter.

In the spring my husband, son, and I flew up for Karen's junior voice recital which was a requirement for voice performance majors. We were surprised to see so many group members and so few classmates at the special occasion. While we were enjoying punch and cookies at the reception, Karen's beloved voice teacher asked to speak to me privately the following day. She told me she had a difficult year with my daughter because Karen seemed unable to focus on music. The teacher remarked that at one point Karen seemed so "out of it" at practice that the teacher had asked Karen if she were on drugs. I'm thankful for this teacher and the staff at the college who understood my concerns and did what they could to get through to my daughter. Unfortunately, the group was a stronger influence.

The campus minister suggested we make some effort to get Karen away from the group. I reasoned that if she were away from the group for any length of time, she would be able to start thinking for herself. My husband and I offered her an all-expense-paid trip abroad where she could stay with her grandparents whom she hadn't seen in years. She was very excited and applied for a passport, but then after talking with her discipler, she told us she had changed her mind about going. Karen stated she couldn't go because there was no church for her to attend there, meaning no International Churches of Christ church.

I was told by cult experts not to attack her church verbally, because to Karen it would be the same as attacking God. But by spring break I was growing impatient with her cult involvement and strange ways, and as a result the two of us spent a lot of time arguing over the phone. In anger, I told her I was investigating her group and I was 100 percent sure it was a destructive cult.

Since we were constantly doing battle, Karen decided not to come home for the summer, but instead to join a caravan of group members who were traveling via cars and vans to San Francisco to replace members there who were starting a mission in the Philippines. For five months, from March until August, we didn't see Karen.

She lived with a family who had been asked to help out in the San Francisco Church of Christ. I was amazed to learn that the man in this family had quit his job as a computer programmer and moved his pregnant wife and two small boys across country to California. There, they lived off savings as he struggled to find employment.

Karen slept on the sofa in the living room of the couple's rented home. She tried to maintain a steady income with job assignments from a temporary employment agency. Later we found out there was tension in the household as the three adults tried to juggle their limited finances in addition to the pressures and demands of the church.

Karen was home for two weeks in August, and then back at school. Her church was recruiting heavily at another college, and Karen told us she was thinking of changing her major to sociology and taking classes there. But my husband and I remained firm that she must finish at the music college. Our fear was that she would quit music altogether and go into the ministry with the group.

In March 1994 we flew up for Karen's senior voice recital. She informed me that she was thinking of not wearing the dress I had bought specifically for her recital. It was a beautiful long, tapered, off-the-shoulders red dress with a slit up the side. The first time Karen had tried it on, she was thrilled, exclaiming it was just perfect for her recital. Because of the group's influence, however, she decided it was too revealing and opted for something more conservative. I strongly protested, telling her that if she didn't wear the dress, then she owed me for it because I didn't like throwing money away.

That night Karen wore the dress, but with the straps pulled up over her shoulders. At the reception no one from her church came up to greet us, but I could sense their curious stares. Karen's few friends from college left early because they felt so out of place with the group members.

A few months later Karen graduated magna cum laude from her college, and her church friends held a nice luncheon for her. It may seem odd, but we really liked her four closest friends from this church, even her discipler! They were very friendly and polite and fun to be with. I saw them as victims, just like Karen—all of them deceived into joining a cult.

Learning to Cope—Hoping for the Future

It has been almost four years since Karen was recruited into the International Churches of Christ, and I have found ways to cope. My minister once told me I would have to learn to accept my daughter the way she is even if it's contrary to how I want her to be. Also, he said letting go doesn't mean giving up. I have tried to turn this over to God, realizing I am powerless over this problem.

Most disturbing to me is the split personality of Karen. One minute she is the happy, vivacious person we once knew, and another minute she is the cult person we don't know at all. The sudden change happens in front of our eyes. It's triggered most often when the conversation turns toward her church. Her voice suddenly becomes very soft and sweet and she speaks in a very condescending way as though she is much wiser than her parents.

Another element of her behavior that I find very disturbing is her notion that she was a very immoral person before she joined this group. The idea that her past lifestyle was very sinful is totally fabricated. In fact, people have often complimented me on raising such a fine, outstanding young person. Karen told me recently that if she had not gotten into this church that today she would be a prostitute or a drug addict. I told her that knowing her character, I knew it was not possible for her to be either one of those, but she said anything is possible. It breaks my heart to know that Karen believes she is susceptible to and protected from some unscrupulous lifestyle by being part of this false religion.

It is puzzling to me that my daughter no longer shows any signs of emotion. She has no laughter, no tears, and no anger. Her temperament remains the same, except during those rare times when the old Karen slips out. It is a great loss to me that the two of us can no longer be close. Before her recruitment Karen was very open and honest, but now she seems to have many secrets and hidden thoughts. Sometimes I feel awkward and self-conscious around her, sensing her disapproval of some of my actions, which she may not consider up to her group's standards.

I have watched her own sense of self-confidence fade as she becomes more and more indecisive, as though afraid to trust her own judgment. Often she will abruptly change her mind after plans have already been set into motion. Even ordering from a menu sometimes becomes a major task for her.

Once when Karen commented to me that she was having a difficult time making a decision, I told her to pray about it. But she said that she does not pray to God for direction in her life, because she doesn't know if the answer is coming from God or Satan since Satan disguises himself as an angel. Then she quoted a scripture from the Bible to back up this belief of hers. Sadly, instead of going to God, she goes to her discipler.

The years of involvement in the group have taken a toll on Karen's health. Not only is she mentally and emotionally abused, but recently she has had several incidents of becoming dizzy and faint. A visit to the doctor confirmed that she is anemic, but with the stress and unrealistic requirements of the group, she has not been able to regain her strength. I fear that the pressures will one day be more than she can endure.

One of the ways I have dealt with this crisis in our family's life is to try to make something good come from something bad. In September 1993 I started a local support group for family members who have a loved one in a cult or other abusive group. It's also open to former cult members who are in the process of recovering from their experiences. We meet once a month to try to find ways of coping with the crisis. I find that it's very therapeutic talking to people who are going through the same thing with their child or other relative.

Through referrals I also talk with people all over the country who are dealing with this issue and offer advice and support. Many times I'm able to refer callers to experts who know more about the particular group they're inquiring about. Occasionally I send information to people calling our support line or I suggest books for them to read.

Over the years my family has tried to maintain a good relationship with Karen. We feel fortunate that she is still allowed contact and visits with us. I try to reinforce in her that our love is unconditional—that we love her no matter what. On the other hand, I remind her that the group members' love is conditional. They love her *only* if she has total commitment, obedience, and loyalty to them.

Someday Karen will remember the values we taught her when she was growing up and she'll realize the group's values aren't consistent with that. We hope that at that time she'll choose to leave. Unfortunately we have no idea when that will be. It could be months or it could be years, but no matter when, we will always be there for her. My husband and I are prepared to help her pick up the pieces of her shattered life and put it back together. I'm as much afraid of her emotional state once she leaves the group as I am now while she is being emotionally abused. There is no way to tell what effect the thought reform and manipulation will have had.

I feel it is very important that parents educate themselves on the techniques of thought reform used by destructive groups and also learn about the particular group their child is involved in. Knowing that what happened to my daughter could happen to others, I plan to do my part to make people aware of this evil plot to snag our bright young people and take away years of their productive lives.

Part IV

A Critical Analysis
of the Boston Movement

12

Exit Counseling and the Boston Movement

Carol Giambalvo

Exit counseling someone who has been involved with the International Churches of Christ[1]—whether in a planned intervention or after the person has left the movement—is a process of presenting information.[2] The goal is to (1) broaden the person's information base and perspective, (2) reawaken critical thinking skills, (3) educate the person about thought reform so that he or she can understand the experience and begin to recover from it,[3] and (4) allow the person to make a

---

[1] The International Churches of Christ has also been known as the Boston Church of Christ, the Boston movement, Multiplying Ministries, Discipling Ministries, and the Crossroads Church of Christ.

[2] For more information on planned interventions and exit counseling, see *Exit Counseling: A Family Intervention* by Carol Giambalvo, and *Recovery from Cults*, edited by M.D. Langone.

[3] Thought reform is a coordinated program of coercive influence and behavior control (see Singer with Lalich, 1995; and Ofshe and Singer, 1986, listed in References at end of chapter).

fully informed decision about continuing involvement in the group.

This chapter is based on my experience as a thought-reform consultant and exit counselor. I have a great deal of experience conducting family interventions with someone involved in one of the Boston movement groups, and I have worked with numerous individuals who left the movement on their own. I have also engaged in extensive research of the movement's leaders, the group dynamics, and the teachings. My research involved a study of the detailed experiences related to me by former members, the group's literature and audiotapes, and books and studies published about the group. I have also attended their services.

Of the former members I've met, most were recruited while in a transition stage in life, the majority as university students. Typically the Boston movement recruits individuals who are among the brightest and the best of their generation. At the time they joined, the movement seemed to offer instant friendships, a sense of belonging to a loving community (eventually replacing their families of origin), a commitment to save the world by evangelizing it for Christ within one generation (i.e., a purpose higher than oneself), and a structure for becoming a mature Christian and living a good, clean, God-centered life. The decision to join was the best decision these individuals could have made given the information presented to them by the group.

After initial contact with the group, and only when group leaders deemed the recruits ready, then one step at a time, the true agenda and internal dynamics of the group were revealed. If these new members questioned, expressed doubt, or rebelled, they were intimidated into conformity through the use of guilt and fear tactics. They were led to believe, and fear, that leaving the movement was equal to leaving God.

Following are highlights of a family intervention with a young man named David (a pseudonym) who was involved with a Boston movement church in the Midwest. Before an intervention is planned, it's necessary to obtain some background information to determine whether an intervention is appropriate or advisable. Some of the background we gathered on this case is provided here.

Background

David was described by his father as a bright, attractive, outgoing nineteen-year-old in his freshman year at a Midwest university. David was in the top 10 percent of his high school graduating class and had spent his junior year abroad as a foreign exchange student. He was active in his family's church's youth fellowship, as well as in extracurricular activities such as golf, volleyball, skiing, and gym. David enjoyed many friendships. He had ended a dating relationship of nine months just before leaving home for college. David was noted to have leadership qualities, a high sense of ethical standards, and a high level of maturity for his age. Family relationships with his parents and teenaged siblings were described as close and loving.

David was recruited into the movement shortly after arriving for his freshman year at college, away from home. When we asked family members why they were concerned, David's father recounted the changes in David's personality and behavior that were noticed by the family. These were as follows:

- The relationship with his best friend from high school, with whom he initially shared a dorm room, became strained once David joined the group. He soon moved out of the dorm and into an apartment with other "brothers" from the group.
- Visits home became much less frequent; when David did come home, he brought other group members with him.
- David no longer engaged in family activities and seemed withdrawn and judgmental.
- David was uninvolved and unemotional about family concerns—a drastic change for him.
- He always seemed exhausted; previously David had enjoyed excellent health, but he had recently been ill.
- David's father suspected that David was not eating properly or getting sufficient sleep.
- David's phone conversations with the family were rushed and unemotional.
- David was always doing some movement activity and was not participating in extracurricular university activities. His father was also concerned about David's ability to maintain his scholastic level.
- David's best friend expressed concern about David to his family. Among other things, the friend said that David tried to get him involved in the group; when he refused, David became extremely judgmental of him.

Family Intervention

The family had hoped things might improve when David came home for the summer. Instead, David took an internship with the movement and did not come home. An intervention was planned for July, when David's father requested that David come home to help with an important project.

Since this voluntary intervention occurred before the movement's warnings to their members about exit counseling and "deprogramming," David was not resistant to his father's plea to talk with us and look at information he had not had access to in the movement. David quickly consented and his father called us into the house. During the first few hours of our meeting, we (a team made up of two exit counselors and a former member of the Boston movement) shared our experiences with David and asked him about his.

It was obvious that David had changed his life goals because of his involvement with the movement. He was now aspiring to go into the full-time "ministry." He planned to pursue courses in a foreign language so that he could be on the movement's "planting team" to start a church in an Eastern European country.

David quickly let us know that his first commitment was to God, and unless we could show him that the movement was not following the Bible and doing God's work, he would always remain in the movement. This was somewhat different from what we usually hear from members. Generally, members tell us that they are committed to the "Kingdom" (the movement says it is the Kingdom of God). His comment gave us an inkling that David's sense of integrity was strong, a very good sign in the beginning of an intervention.

Although we saw the usual signs of defensiveness and denial in David, they came up only occasionally. We also noted periods early on when he could think critically and interact with the information being presented to him.

David said he was attracted to the group because the person who had approached him seemed outgoing, with

189

interests similar to his. The first event David attended was a Bible Talk. He felt drawn to the Bible study as well as the people in the group, who appeared to live what they believed and have a strong sense of purpose in doing God's will. David expressed that he was flattered by the attention shown to him at the Bible Talk and again afterward when other members called him and invited him to movies, to play sports, and to other group activities.

David was shocked when we showed him the movement's "14-Day Plan," which revealed that group leaders discuss potential new members and assign them three to six "friends." The role of these friends is to ensure that the recruit begins an individual Bible study and gets baptized (the role played by these "friends" is an example of Lifton's theme of mystical manipulation[4]). Even though later on David himself attended leadership meetings, the manipulativeness of this technique had not occurred to him. The group had justified it as just a way of helping people get to God. Now he could see it in another light.

We then went over the movement's other workbooks on leadership, showing David how leaders are instructed to study potential new members and assess how best to convert them by "changing their hearts" (Lifton's loading the language) and to determine how fast recruits can be led to that change. We looked at the labels used to categorize potential members according to how quickly or slowly they are able to

---

[4] Throughout this description of the discussions, parenthetical comments will indicate when a point fits one of Margaret Singer's six conditions for a thought-reform environment (see Appendix A) or one of Robert Lifton's eight psychological themes (see Appendix B).

pursue pre-baptismal studies: labels such as back burner, front burner, crock pot, in the oven, and microwave.

Members are instructed to get potential converts to study as often as possible, to get them baptized quickly, and, simultaneously, to build great friendships by encouraging converts, being there for them, and helping them in any way possible, and having fun times together (Singer's condition 1).

Although the pre-baptismal study is called an individual Bible study, it is conducted in meetings with two members and one recruit (Singer's condition 1). One person leads the study while the other takes notes for the recruit. By going over the content of the pre-baptismal studies we demonstrated to David how the studies are designed—step by step and using scripture out of context (Singer's conditions 1 & 5)—to narrow recruits' options to the point that they are convinced that they were never Christian before, that the only Christians are in the Boston movement, and that in order to truly follow God they must be baptized as a disciple into the movement and be fully committed to all movement activities, services, and "gatherings of the body." Members must evangelize daily and bring in new converts, and constantly seek advice from their discipling partner (Singer's condition 5; Lifton's demand for purity). A discipling partner is a person who is assigned to the new member and is "over him or her in the Lord." Everyone—except Kip McKean, the leader of the movement—is required to have a discipling partner.

With the aid of textbooks and guidelines from mainstream Christianity, using many sources and perspectives, we contrasted the Boston movement's techniques with healthy, proper conversion procedures and Bible study safeguards. At this point we spent several hours studying and discussing Dr. Margaret Singer's conditions for thought reform. We read about and discussed Ericksonian hypnosis and its use in religious cult conversion processes. We looked at and discussed videos that describe and demonstrate hypnosis and other methods of trance induction.

A trance state is one in which an individual's attention is centrally focused to the exclusion of peripheral awareness. Simultaneously, a special relationship exists between the person inducing the trance and the subject. In this special relationship, generally the subject views the other as someone more spiritual, more enlightened, with something of much value to offer. A transient mild trance state can be achieved without a formal trance induction; the speaker or leader does not need to announce that he or she is "doing hypnosis" (Miller, 1986; Singer, 1985).

We read and discussed at length two chapters from Flavil Yeakley's book, *The Discipling Dilemma* (1988). Yeakley gave 835 members of the Boston Church of Christ the Myers-Briggs Type Indicator (MBTI), a psychological test that classifies people according to psychologist Carl Jung's type system. The premise is that individuals differ in the way in which they tend to perceive (sense oriented vs. intuition oriented), the way they judge (thinking vs. feeling), and in their basic attitudes (extroversion vs. introversion). Isabel Myers and Katherine Briggs, the developers of the MBTI, added another dimension to Jung's typology: that is, a person's preferred way of orienting herself or himself to the outside world. This orientation may be judging or perceiving. The MBTI thus allows for sixteen personality types based on permutations of these variables.

Yeakley asked subjects to answer the MBTI questions in the following ways: (1) as they thought they would have answered before their conversion into the Boston church, (2) as they felt at the time of testing, and (3) as they thought they would answer after five more years of discipling with the movement. He found that "a great majority of the members of the Boston Church of Christ changed psychological type scores in the past, present, and future versions of the MBTI" (p.34) and that "the observed changes in psychological type scores were not random since there was a clear convergence in a single type" (p.35). The type toward which members converged was that of the group's leader. Comparisons with tests of members of mainstream denominations showed no convergence, whereas tests of members of other cultic groups did show convergence, although toward different types than that on which the Boston church members converged.

From this study Yeakley concludes that "there is a group dynamic operating in that congregation that influences members to change their personalities to conform to the group norm" (p. 37). Although Yeakley's study did not directly examine harm, it does indirectly support clinical observations that contend that cult members' personalities are molded to fit the group. During this discussion David's father talked about his worry about some of the personality changes the family had observed in David.

David was impressed with the results of Yeakley's research. He expressed concern that personality changes due to environmental pressures to conform are unhealthy for an individual. He told us that he never had a problem with having to change as much as he saw others change since he was an extrovert before joining the group. But one of his disciples had a problem because he was a natural introvert and David had been encouraged by leadership to apply more pressure on the disciple to "die to the sin" of being "inwardly focused" and to push himself to reach out to others in order to bring them into the church (Singer's condition 4). Previously, David viewed the challenges and confrontations to individuals' behavior and attitudes as "helping them to become better Christians"; he had welcomed these challenges when they came in his direction. Our discussion allowed David to view such pressures to conform in a new light.

How the Teachings Coincide with Thought Reform

Almost as soon as we had discussed the movement's pressure to conform at length, David immediately vacillated, saying that a Christian's first concern should be saving souls and winning the world for Christ. He talked in terms of being fruitful. The movement's definition of *fruit* is new converts.

At this point we did a study of the term and looked at some of the movement's printed materials on leadership qualifications. We contrasted them with the qualifications for leadership that are biblical and found no reference to fruitfulness, especially in terms of the movement's use of the word (Lifton's loading the language).

This discussion helped David to once again see the movement's distortion of scripture. He was thinking clearly again and eager to continue the examination. David turned his attention to the issue of personality change.

We discussed this, reviewing Singer's analysis of the use of older group members as models for the new behavior that leadership wants to bring about in new members. David told us that he had been encouraged to imitate his discipling partner, so we went over the group's teachings on imitation. He was incredulous when we read a tape transcript about one leader in the movement who was chastised for not liking to drink coffee: his discipler drank coffee, and the leader was to imitate his discipler in all ways (Singer's conditions 3 & 4).

In discussing how the imitation principle works all the way up the pyramidal structure, David was able to combine Singer's principle with the results of Yeakley's research. He saw how the accusation is arrived at that people in the movement are being cloned in the image of Kip McKean.

While addressing the imitation principle and personality change, we also discussed the pyramidal structure of the movement (Singer's condition 6). We drew a diagram for David, beginning with him and his disciples underneath him, then going up to his discipling partner, and on up the ladder to the lead evangelist in his church. Then we drew a diagram showing how each church leader is discipled by another church leader, up the ladder to the World Sector Leaders, who are each discipled by McKean.

When David saw the final diagram, he commented, "It's definitely a pyramid. And Kip sure is at the top." David remarked that when he was baptized, he had not known that the church was part of the Boston Church of Christ movement (Singer's condition 6).

Now we discussed the characteristics of cults and the fact that most cult leaders are self-appointed. We discussed McKean's background and also looked at the process by which mainstream Christian ministers and priests are educated and ordained. We examined some of McKean's own negativity toward credentials as expressed in transcriptions of his talks and sermons.

We turned our attention back to the discipling relationship, discussing the manipulation of the disciple's guilt and fear and how that relates to the confession process. Disciples are required to "seek advice" from their discipler about all matters and, simultaneously, be "open" about themselves. This openness includes confessing any "sin" or "bad attitudes" toward the movement or leadership (Lifton's cult of confession). Initially David had looked at this as helping an individual to become a better Christian. But after these discussions he was more readily able to see the controlling aspect of the system. After we viewed videos of how other cults use these same methods with similar rationalizations, David was convinced.

In looking at this kind of system in contrast to the Bible's books of Galatians and Romans 14, David saw that not only was the methodology manipulative, but also that the movement had placed itself between him and God, and had interpreted for him what God wanted of him (Lifton's mystical manipulation). It occurred to David that he had set aside his own career goals, his own interests, talents, and creativity to become what the movement told him he needed to be for God. He told us that he had been seriously considering studying in Europe for a year, but had been forbidden from doing so by the movement's campus minister because there was no movement church in the particular location David would have been going to (Lifton's milieu control; Singer's condition 3).

Prior to joining the group David had signed up and paid for a ski trip sponsored by a university ski club. After his baptism, he was told unequivocally not to go. He was convinced by his discipler that if he went on the trip he would somehow "fall into sin" and fall away from the church (Lifton's demand for purity & milieu control; Singer's conditions 1, 2 & 3).

David told us that at one point he had questioned the way a scripture was being taught and was told by leadership that he had better "study it out." When study didn't clear up his question, but instead intensified it, David presented the question to leadership again. This time he was told that he had a bad attitude and needed to "look at his own heart" (Singer's condition 5; Lifton's sacred science & demand for purity).

He was also told that if the Bible Talk he was leading didn't have guests, if he wasn't studying with people and getting them baptized, then there was sin in the lives of the Bible Talk members—they weren't "cranking" (Lifton's loading the language). The pressure had been put on David to get the people in his Bible Talk back in line. Goals were set for how many new converts each Bible Talk, or zone, was to have within certain periods of time (zones are now called sectors). As a result David spent practically all of his time during school semesters on group activities. He found that he had to study and fulfill course requirements by staying up late and getting less sleep. He was constantly under pressure, but learned to deny it even to himself because he had to be a "happy Christian" so as to bring others "to the Lord" (Lifton's doctrine over person).

David initiated a discussion of the issue of dating, so we explored the movement's teachings on dating. When we looked at the dating guidelines in a church bulletin, David was incredulous. He said, "We jokingly called the dating guidelines the 'Pharisee's list.' But there really is one!" Even though he knew all the dating rules, he had never before actually seen them in print.

Questions and Doubts

During his summer internship David had led Bible Talks, conducted more individual studies with potential members, attended more leadership meetings, and discipled more members (Singer's condition 2). The intensity increased. Yet in fleeting moments when David allowed himself to consider that "something is wrong here," he quickly felt disloyal and guilty (Lifton's demand for purity; Singer's condition 5), and was afraid that Satan was somehow "getting a foothold" (Lifton's loading the language). So David's doubts were placed on a shelf somewhere in the corner of his mind.

It got to a point where David no longer had conscious doubts because he had to confess them to his discipler and then get an attitude adjustment (Lifton's cult of confession; Singer's condition 5). David began to suppress and deny such thoughts so that he wouldn't be humiliated in front of other leaders and possibly be removed from a leadership position (Lifton's demand for purity; Singer's conditions 3 & 5).

The movement's admonition that "If you leave this church, you are leaving God" became the ultimate threat and fear for David (Lifton's dispensing of existence; Singer's condition 5). He felt there was nowhere else to go. Leaders talked continually of people who "fell away from the church" and "fell back into sin" or had something terrible happen to them (Lifton's loading the language & dispensing of existence). Often, when someone left the movement, leadership would say it was because of a particular sin, and they would then name the sin that the person had "struggled with" most during confessions.

David talked about how members' attitudes and sins were openly discussed at leadership meetings. The rationale was that disciplers needed to "seek advice" on how to handle their disciplees and give them advice. Potential new members were also openly discussed: how they were progressing, what needed to be done to more quickly and effectively move them toward baptism, what was going on in their lives, and who should be assigned to "help them" (Lifton's mystical manipulation; Singer's conditions 1, 2, & 3).

When David began to share these examples with us, it showed that he was thinking critically and making connections. At this point, even though David verbalized that he needed to leave the movement, we did an in-depth study of Lifton's criteria for thought reform. David was able to give us examples from his own experience in the movement for each of Lifton's criteria.

We then discussed the possibility that David might experience triggers (reminders of his time in the movement) and flashback occurrences, which are quite common after someone leaves such a group (Tobias & Lalich, 1994). We also explored some options for David regarding the issue of whether or how to inform the group that he was leaving.

When he went back to school in the fall, David spoke out about the movement and helped warn others who were becoming involved. Later he assisted in several family interventions. David is doing well. He now has a master's degree in business and is employed in a good position. He is now married to another former member of the movement, and they are attending a church of their own choice.

References

Carol Giambalvo. *Exit Counseling: A Family Intervention.* Bonita Springs, FL: AFF, 1995.

Michael D. Langone, Ed. *Recovery from Cults: help for Victims of Psychological and Spiritual Abuse.* New York: W.W. Norton, 1993.

Robert J. Lifton. *Thought Reform and the Psychology of Totalism.* Chapel Hill: University of North Carolina, 1989.

Jesse Miller. "The Utilization of Hypnotic Techniques in Religious Conversion." *Cultic Studies Journal,* 1986, 3(2), 243–250.

Richard Ofshe and Margaret T. Singer. "Attacks on Peripheral versus Central Elements of Self and the Impact of Thought Reforming Techniques." *Cultic Studies Journal,* 1986, 3(1), 3–24.

Margaret Thaler Singer with Janja Lalich. *Cults in Our Midst: The Hidden Menace in Our Everyday Lives.* San Francisco: Jossey-Bass, 1995.

Madeleine Landau Tobias and Janja Lalich. *Captive Hearts, Captive Minds: Freedom and Recovery from Cults and Abusive Relationships.* Alameda, CA: Hunter House, 1994.

Flavil Yeakley. *The Discipling Dilemma.* Nashville, TN: Gospel Advocate Co., 1988.

13

An Examination of the Boston Movement in Relation to Thought-Reform Criteria

Carol Giambalvo

Psychiatrist Robert J. Lifton, while working for the U.S. Army, began studying the techniques used by the North Koreans on prisoners of war. He also studied the techniques used in the Communist Chinese reeducation program in their "revolutionary universities." In 1961 the first edition of his book *Thought Reform and the Psychology of Totalism* was published. In Chapter 22, Lifton lists eight psychological themes that constitute a thought-reform program or environment.

Lifton states that his eight criteria "were meant to provide principles of a general kind, criteria for evaluating any environment in relationship to ideological totalism. Such patterns are all too readily embraced by a great variety of groups, large and small, as a means of manipulating human beings, always in the name of higher purpose (1989, p. viii).

The comparison done here focuses on the Boston movement's use of thought-reform techniques to recruit and retain members. It addresses the social and psychological methods used to achieve that end. These methods are similar in nature to those employed by many well-known cults, regardless of their content or ideology.

THE BOSTON MOVEMENT

I have drawn from the interviews and personal accounts in the preceding chapters, comparing their experiences in the movement to the eight psychological themes identified by Lifton as ideological totalism. Some examples may fall into more than one category, as the criteria are closely related and interdependent. The names in parentheses following each example indicate the interview or account from which the material was drawn. Other sources of information and data used here are the movement's writings and teachings found in bulletins and *Upside Down* magazine (formerly known as *Discipleship*), as well as audiotapes of seminars, workshops, and sermons.

I wish to make clear that it is the methodology of the movement that is being examined and critiqued, not the doctrine, nor the intentions of the majority of its members. As Lifton states, "Thought reform has a psychological momentum of its own, a self-perpetuating energy not always bound by the interests of the program's directors" (1989, p. 419). While the initial goals of the movement's founders may have been good, the use of thought reform results in nothing less than totalism. As the thought-reform system gains momentum, more control and more justification becomes necessary. The leaders or founders then take on "the end justifies the means" philosophy and use more and more control.

All of the former members I have worked with have been sincere and intelligent. They learned a system of communication and a dynamic of interaction that is highly manipulative; they were victims of that system. Many cult members end up being both victims and perpetrators, which is why a focus on the thought-reform system most effectively helps former members recover from their experience and move on with their lives.

Milieu Control

Milieu control is the control of communication within an environment. It seeks to limit all forms of communication with the outside world by attempting to control what a person hears, sees, writes, expresses, and experiences. If the control is intense, it ultimately becomes an internalized control—that is, an attempt to manage an individual's inner communication with himself. If successful, the group no longer has to exert total control of the exterior environment. An individual is turned against his or her own inner voice in order to dispel any doubts about the group or the leader. Individual autonomy becomes a threat to the group.

Milieu control is maintained through intense peer pressure with the only validating feedback coming from group members, continuous psychological pressure, and isolation via geographical and/or psychological distance from other people, information, or ideas outside the belief system of the group. There is often a sequence of events or training, such as seminars, lectures, and group encounters, which becomes increasingly intense and increasingly isolated, making it extremely difficult, both physically and psychologically, for a person to leave.

Intense milieu control can contribute to a dramatic change of identity, which Lifton calls "doubling": the formation of a second self (the ideal cult personality) that lives side by side with the precult self, often for a considerable time. When the milieu control is lifted, elements of the earlier self generally surface.

Cults tend to become islands of totalism within a larger society. This situation can create a dynamic of its own, for in order to maintain the milieu control, cult leaders must often intensify their rules and regulations, increase their range of control, and manage the environment more systematically, and sometimes with greater intensity. Cult leaders are often forced to find ways by which to isolate members from critical information offered by the outside world, especially when media coverage mounts.

Examples

- There is an attempt to get potential converts to study the Bible in pre-baptismal study as often as possible and to baptize them quickly. (David, Nina, Michael, Edgar, Mary, Shalon)

- Potential converts are encouraged to do individual Bible study (pre-baptismal study) without being told that the goal of this study is to get them baptized into membership. The study is actually a two-on-one situation: one person leads the study, another takes notes for the recruit. Often a leader is brought in for the Counting the Costs session. (David, Nina, Michael, Edgar, Mary, Shalon)

- In effect, the group will isolate people from family and friends. For example, Mary was psychologically isolated from her husband early on in their marriage.

- Members of the group convinced Mary that she was being persecuted at home and praised her for her perseverance. Later, they made her a heroine for surviving an exit counseling.

- Women in Challenging Situations is a support group for women married to "non-Christian" men in the New York City Church of Christ. It teaches that the more difficult the trial a woman endures, the more faithful and spiritual she is in the eyes of God. (Mary)

- Members are encouraged to move out of existing living arrangements and to move in with other movement sisters or brothers. (David, Mary, James, Edgar, Michael)
- Time commitments required by the group isolate members from prior support systems. (David, Mary, James, Sally, Nina, Michael, Shalon)
- Mary did not even have time to think about her husband, family, or outside friends, as the movement's control over her had been so locked in (internalized).
- It is taught that safe people (members) are obedient to God and are saved; unsafe people (nonmembers) are damned to hell and are dangerous to associate with. (Michael, David)
- Becoming a member requires breaking up dating relationships with nonmembers. (Michael)
- Members are advised not to move to a geographical location that does not have a discipling church (movement church). (James, David, Michael)
- Edgar related, "Once I moved into the apartment (with members), I found myself answering to the church for everything I did."
- Members are convinced by the group that their parents are trying to control them when the parents criticize the church or question the amount of time their son or daughter spends with the group. (Sally, Mary)
- The amount of time a member must spend doing group activities causes serious problems in studies, job performance, and family relations. (Michael, David, Mary)
- Emotionally, group members become "family," replacing family of origin. (Michael, Mary)

- When Mary thought of seeking marriage counseling, she was told by group leaders, "You know what kind of advice you will receive from a worldly counselor."
- Members are warned about media persecution to disarm or dispel the criticism and desensitize members. Criticism of the movement gets redefined as persecution. (Mary, Michael)
- The group conducts studies about public and family persecution. (Michael)
- The group warns members in sermons, teachings, and magazine articles about "deprogramming" and instills fear into members' relationship with parents and family. (Mary)
- An article appearing in the movement's magazine *Upside Down* in January 1993 gave information about deprogramming and warned members to be wary of their parents. It warned: "If your family is distressed by the direction your life has taken, you are at least a possible candidate for a surprise intervention. The best prevention is to avoid the situation altogether." In the same article Kip McKean (leader of the movement) advised members to view deprogrammings as spiritual pornography.
- Members are warned not to look at information that is critical of the group. Such information is deemed "spiritual pornography." (Mary)
- When Shalon had a question about an article that was critical of the movement, the Women's Counselor laid the magazine and the Bible side by side and asked Shalon, "Which one are you going to listen to?"
- "You know there is a proliferation—literally, that's the word—of not only anti-cult material, little packets, booklets, books, videos—Preston Sheppard calls this stuff spiritual pornography. You say, well, 'why?' Well, what was

206

the reason you first opened *Playboy* magazine? You were curious. You know, a lot of us as Christians, we don't understand the schemes of Satan. How did Satan get Eve? By her curiosity. Just twisting a few things around. Even the world says curiosity kills the cat. Some of you say, 'Well, hold it. If you are strong enough, if there isn't anything wrong in this stuff, then why shouldn't I read these anti-Boston materials?' Well, let me ask you this. You've been a Christian for a while and prayerfully, you're strong in the Lord. Why can't you just open a *Playboy* and just see how it goes? Let me tell you something, I have been a Christian for 17 years. I don't dare get close to one! And you shouldn't get close to that spiritual pornography. The thing that is driving you there is curiosity. That is Satan. Get it out of the house!" (Kip McKean, "They Hated the Dreamer")

• Following an unsuccessful attempt at a voluntary family intervention Mary was protected from her husband and family by the group.

Mystical Manipulation (Planned Spontaneity)

Mystical manipulation is a systematic process by which events are planned and managed by leadership but appear to have arisen spontaneously. In the Bible-based groups these events often give the appearance that the group or the leaders are very spiritual or God-inspired. To members or new recruits, it rarely feels like manipulation. Techniques such as fasting, chanting, singing, and limited sleep are used by some groups to produce an altered state of consciousness in the members, which heightens the effectiveness of planned spontaneity.

Mystical manipulation can take on a special quality because cult leaders become intermediaries for God: a particular "chosen" human being is seen as a source of

207

salvation or able to give individual members the "only truth," the "only path to salvation." Such God-centered principles are put forth forcibly and claimed exclusively, so that the cult, the leader, and the beliefs become the only true path to salvation. This can give intensity to the mystical manipulation and provide a rationalization for those promoting it.

If there is a specific individual who becomes the center of the mystical manipulation, a twofold process comes into play. The leader can sometimes be more real than an abstract god and therefore attainable to cult members. On the other hand, that person can also be a source of disillusionment.

Mystical manipulation can also legitimize deception (it becomes acceptable to deceive or not be totally open and truthful with the outside world). Those who have not "seen the light," who are not in the realm of the cult, are considered to be in the realm of evil. and therefore can be justifiably deceived for the higher purpose (of saving them or exploiting them to the cult's benefit). For example, a group may use a different name (front name) for recruitment purposes, especially if media exposure has caused people to be wary. Or it may become acceptable to invite people to a cult gathering without letting them know that the real purpose is to get them to join the group. It is all right not to let recruits know the ultimate (hidden) agenda of the group. The totalistic ideology can, and often does, justify such deception (that is, the end justifies the means).

Examples
• During the pre-baptismal study, prospective members are convinced that the group is *the* Kingdom of God. (David, Mary, Shalon)

- The leaders of the movement are believed to have a special relationship with God. (Mary)
- "Your leadership is determinate [sic] on who you are married to. You need to appreciate who you are married to. You are married to God's special boys, the sons of whom he derives the greatest joy." (Kip McKean, "Be Perfectly United")
- "And you say, 'I've not grumbled against God.' Listen, if you have grumbled against any of God's leaders, you have grumbled against God." (Kip McKean, "Be Perfectly United")
- Mary sincerely believed that God was leading the movement.
- "We, the church, are the Kingdom of God." (Kip McKean, "Revolution Through Restoration," *Upside Down*, 2, 1992)
- "In the many churches where there was no desire to help, an obligation to God was felt to call out the true disciples and ask them to move to the 'Boston churches,' preferably called 'multiplying ministry churches.' Thus we set about gleaning the remnant into what was clearly now a movement of God." (Kip McKean, "Ten Year Report")
- "Kip McKean is the greatest living treasure that God has given the Kingdom on the face of the earth today.... The influence of a man like this, just like the influence of a Peter, John, Titus, or a Paul, cannot be limited to one place or one situation. That influence must be free to range throughout the world, and to be used by God all over the world. That is the decision that has been made tonight...It is the greatest moment in the Kingdom that I have seen in about 15 years." (Sam Laing, movement evangelist, "Kip McKean Enters Full-Time Mission Work," *Discipleship*, Summer, 1988)

- Members are told that their disciplers are placed "over them in the Lord" by God.
- "Also, we need to trust in God completely to enable us to grow and, most importantly, we need to trust the people he has put in our life to help us change. Ultimately, if we do not trust these people, we do not trust God. To the extent that I trust my discipler, Gloria Baird, I am in reality trusting God." (Theresa Ferguson, Women's Counselor, in BCC bulletin, "Forever Growing," Oct. 22, 1989)
- Because of the movement's "amazing" growth, members are told that God is in charge of the movement. (Michael)
- "We serve a super God who works in supernatural ways in order to produce supernatural results. We are not a movement of men. We are THE movement of God." (Kip McKean: "The Dream—Super Churches," 1992)
- Members are led to believe that no other clergy or religions have the truth. The truth can only be found in this movement. (Michael, Nina, James, Edgar, Mary, Sally)
- The movement's plan for world evangelism is deemed God's plan: "God's plan is clear. We have our marching orders—into all nations! Therefore, the plan we must adopt is clear—get into all nations! Our goal as a movement is to accomplish this by the year 2000. We must go, make disciples, baptizing them and teaching them to obey all that Jesus commanded—in all nations! Boston was the modern day movement's birthplace that God used through the visionary ministry of my brother, Kip, and his wife, Elena, to begin planting discipling churches in all areas of the world." (Randy McKean, in BCC bulletin, "Into ALL Nations," May 23, 1993)

- "Therefore, in the presence of God and Christ Jesus who will judge the living and the dead and in view of his appearing and his kingdom we give you this charge: Give to God your dreams, energies, health, finances, intellects, families, and yes even your life, to plant churches in the remaining 111 nations by the year 2000." ("The Evangelization Proclamation," signed by all the World Sector Leaders, Feb. 4, 1994)
- Potential members are deceived by being invited to a nondenominational Bible study (Bible Talk) instead of being told that it is part of a movement and that the Bible Talk is really a recruitment tool. (Edgar, Michael, James)
- On college campuses the group uses names such as Campus Advance, Alpha Omega, Christians on Campus, Christian Associates, CU, IMPACT, CROSS, Students for Christ.
- Once a person attends a Bible Talk, the leadership discusses each person and assigns three to six "friends" to that person, according to his or her needs. Potential recruits think they have found a wonderful group of "friendly" people who care about them. They think it happened spontaneously, and have no idea that all the phone calls and social invitations were carefully planned without their knowledge. (David, James, Shalon, Edgar, Michael)
- Potential recruits' progress is discussed openly in leadership meetings. (David, Mary)
- In the following quotation from a leadership retreat study, the term *smart studying* refers to the prebaptismal studies conducted with potential members. The terms *crock pot* and so forth are defined by estimated time periods until the individual will be baptized. From "Countdown to Leadership Study: SECRET #5: Smart Studying":

211

A. Study the Person, Not the Study
  1. Crock Pot—more than six weeks
  2. Back Burner—three to six weeks
  3. Front Burner—within three weeks
  4. In the Oven—any day now
  5. Microwave—less than a week start to finish
B. Gang Tackle the Open Visitor
C. Focus on the Most Open Person
D. Move Studies Quickly—Three Weeks Average
E. Build a Great Friendship
F. Must be willing to confront
G. Be Aware of Existing Close Relationships
H. More than one Person in on Study
  1. Never less than two or more than three
I. Keep Leadership Informed on Progress (maybe get them in on the study)

• Mary thought that the friendship between her and the Tanners had arisen spontaneously. Actually, it was arranged without her knowledge.

• Mary gave an example of assigning a sister to a visitor who worked on Sunday and could not attend Sunday services. The sister was one who had been in that situation but decided that God's work came before her job. This illustrates how "friends" are selected for potential converts according to their "needs."

• Detailed plans were made for each visitor attending a Bible Talk. The plans included who would be the potential new member's friends, who would conduct the pre-baptismal study with them, and so on. This was done without the knowledge of the visitor. (Mary)

• The attitudes and sins of members are discussed openly in leaders' meetings. (David)

- Mary learned to be totally submissive and obedient to leaders, to disassociate herself from her family and husband, and, at the same time, to deceive and manipulate unsuspecting people—supposedly all in the service of a loving God.
- When visitors came, members behaved in an overly friendly manner. (Edgar, James, Shalon)
- Social events and parties are used to recruit new members deceptively. (Edgar, Michael, Shalon)
- Michael's discipler warned him not to volunteer for Campus Life because God did not want him to do that. He was told that God wanted him to reach out to Vanderbilt students.
- Edgar was told that God worked to bring him back to the group after he left and later returned.
- The inordinate amount of time that is spent on group activities can cause members to get less and less sleep. (Michael, David, Mary, Shalon)
- Members are encouraged to fast if they are struggling with a decision or a problem. At times the leadership calls everyone to fast for a particular purpose.

Demand for Purity

The demand for purity calls for a radical separation of pure and impure, of good and evil, of saved and not saved, of the group and of the world, within an environment and within each individual. Absolute purification is a never-ending process. Members must purge from themselves and from their environment anything that does not conform to the group's beliefs and practices. In such an environment a "snitch" is easily put into place, with members reporting "sins" of nonconformity to leaders. Within an individual this is enforced by the call for constant self-monitoring and confession, which becomes a source of guilt and shame. Guilt and shame are induced in the members in order to gain control over them. This is often done within a specific confessional process that has its own structure, sometimes via mutual criticism and self-criticism in small groups.

The individual comes to apply the same totalist polarization of good and evil to his judgments of his own character: he tends to credit certain aspects of himself with excessive virtue, and condemn even more excessively other personal qualities—all according to their standing within the group. He must look at his impurities as originating from outside influences—that is, from the ever-threatening outside world or Satanic forces. Therefore, one of the best ways to relieve himself of some of his burden of guilt is to denounce those outside influences. Once an individual has experienced this totalist polarization of good and evil, he has great difficulty in regaining a more balanced inner sensitivity to the complexities of human morality. Even after leaving a cult, individuals find it difficult to eliminate the black-and-white, all-or-nothing thinking.

Examples

• Members must be fully committed to all of the group's activities. (David, Mary, James, Michael, Shalon)
• Members must "reach out" (recruit/evangelize) daily. (David, Mary, James, Sally, Edgar)
• Being successful at bringing in new converts results in leadership positions. (Mary, David)
• Every member must have a discipler (discipleship partner). (all)

- "But, at the very outset, we need to establish that discipleship, making disciples, being a disciple, being discipled and discipling others is not an option." (Tom Brown, "Teach Them to Obey")
- Members are taught to imitate their discipler and leaders. (David, Michael, Mary)
- From Countdown to Leadership Study: SECRET #8: Imitate Your Leaders:

I. Introduction
  A. Quickest way to grow is to imitate and be a great disciple
II. Being a Great Disciple
  A. Honesty with discipler
    1. Vs. shading the truth, lying, people-pleasing, wanting to look good
  B. A great reaction to correction
    1. Vs. defensiveness, anger, pouting, self-pity, blame shifting, rationalizing
  C. Openness about feelings and emotions
  D. Realize that God has put discipler there
  E. Have a humble, submissive attitude
  F. Have an agenda when you get together
  G. Decide to imitate—interactions, Bible Talk leading, studies, "what would my discipler do here?"
  H. Learn to think and reason like your discipler

- "Let me tell you this, the people that are easiest to disciple are those individuals who are the ones who most want to imitate you. Because the moment you start saying, 'Well, there are some parts about this brother that I am a little bit unsure of,' what that person begins to do is they begin to filter through the direction and advice that's given to them. And when they start filtering through, they begin to filter out. And when they start filtering out, they're going to filter out what seems best to them, and the whole point of being a disciple is that they don't know what is best for them. But their discipler knows what is best for them. And so I believe a challenge for us is to say, 'Listen, I really love and appreciate my Zone leader. But more than that, I want to be like him.'" (Kip McKean, teaching a class at the 1988 Leadership Retreat)

• "I believe that the disciples need to follow even personality traits. I think disciples need to imitate us wholly in what we do. I think we need to call disciples to do that." (Scott Green, at the 1988 Leadership Conference)

• "And Marty said, 'You've just been a lousy disciple.' And it's true. I haven't imitated him 100% And I believe in imitation. I teach it. But I know Marty's right. And Marty, I apologize to you before the church. And I thank you for that." (Dave Weger, at San Diego Church Revival, Sept. 18, 1992. Weger was lead evangelist in the San Diego church; Marty Fuqua, a World Sector Leader brought in to lead the revival.)

• David was told he could not go on a university club ski trip because he might fall into sin.

• If members make a decision without first seeking advice from their discipler, they often feel guilty. (Michael, Shalon)

• If a Bible Talk is not having enough guests, there is something wrong with the members or the leader, some spiritual shortcoming. (David, Mary)

• The group has rules for dating. (David, Mary, Nina, Michael, Shalon)

• The following excerpts are taken from a dating devotional study given by Frank Kim, Oct. 9, 1987 [Note:

only those who are members of the movement are considered "Christians"]:

> The Dating Scene: Who should I ask out?
> <u>Christians</u>.
> Why?
> Because you usually end up marrying who you date.
> Special consideration for those who want to go into the ministry. You need to look for sisters who are spiritual. You need to marry somebody who can make it in the ministry.
> Expressing Affection:
> Kissing: once per date. Usually only after you're going steady. Don't French kiss.
> Hand holding: Think about it. A lot is communicated. Guard yourselves even after you're going steady.
> Hugs: A good, warm, brotherly hug. Watch that you don't stumble and get too affectionate here.
> Single vs. Double Dating:
> Double date because it helps you to stay pure.
> How often can brothers and sisters call each other on the phone?
> No strict rules, but get advice. Once a week is a good guideline.

• If a member allows himself or herself to think "something is wrong here," it is accompanied by guilt and feelings of disloyalty. (David, Mary, Shalon)
• Shalon was told it is a sin to be attracted to someone outside the church.
• "Reconstructions" of members (and churches) occur to determine commitment levels and weed out those not totally committed. Members are asked whether they have any

unspoken attitudes or criticism of leaders, any unconfessed sin, and so forth. (Mary, Michael)

• The following are notes containing the questions a person leading the reconstruction study would ask a disciple:

Reconstruction Questions

A. What are the best/worst things about your childhood? (Be specific. Ask deep questions.)

  1. Ask about specific feelings (i.e., rejection, insecurity, not loved).

  2. Who did you get your needs met by?

  3. Ask about specific situations (i.e., sexual and physical abuse).

B. Ask specific questions about sexual involvement. When did you start? How many? (Be very specific in this area. Ask for examples.)

C. How do you feel about the church? (i.e., attitudes, quiet reservations)

  1. Qualms about the leaders. Who and why?

  2. Unresolved tensions with DP and other Christians.

  3. Do you think the Boston Church is from God? Do you think you are of God?

D. If you were to rate your baptism on a scale of 1–10 (1 being the greatest doubt), where would you put yourself?

E. Do you have any bad attitudes or hurts from the past? What are they? Have you ever told anyone?

F. Go to Gal. 5:19 and ask specific questions about sin, the sins repented of before baptism and after? Did you confess all your sins before you were baptized?

  1. What do you consider your biggest sin now?

G. Have you ever converted anybody?

H. Have you ever been tempted with homosexuality? Challenge on.

Critical Perspectives

    I. Is there anything you have not been open about, or anything you do not have a clear conscience about?

    J. What would Jesus say about your life?

        1. Do you think you are a Christian? If not, why not?

- Mary was convinced by church leaders that by remaining with her husband, Tom, she was not trusting God.
- Members in leadership positions have to maintain an excessive time schedule which often leads to exhaustion, skipping meals, neglect of studies, giving up all former interests and pursuit of talents, which eventually can lead to illness. (Mary, David, James, Shalon)
- Members are made to feel guilty for questioning or having criticisms. They are told that if they are doing so, they don't have a disciple's heart, that they are being rebellious or independent. (Nina, Shalon)
- "Listen, if you've grumbled against any of God's leaders, you have grumbled against God." (Kip McKean, "Be Perfectly United")
- When "seeking advice" from disciplers, members are often put in a double bind. They are asked, "Is this a Kingdom decision?"—meaning is it seeking the Kingdom first? James was offered an opportunity to teach music at a summer camp which meant he could not attend church that summer. After being advised that he had better pray over his decision, he decided to take the position. Then his discipler told him he had not prayed hard enough and, later, James was confronted harshly. After being confronted James decided not to take the position. However, during a group session, his discipler chastised him for not making a "pure" decision because he had to be talked out of his original decision.

219

THE BOSTON MOVEMENT

This is an example of how direct orders often will not be given, but there really is no choice for the individual. He or she must either please God (the group) or please himself or herself (selfish, sin). The group sets the standard of behavior for all to conform to and then deems it "God's will for you." Under these conditions, however, it is very difficult for members to see that they are being controlled. They *feel* as though they are only being "advised" and are making their own decisions.

- Edgar related: "Each day I would have to explain my actions, how I used my time, whom I had talked to, and whether I had won any new converts for the church."
- In the pre-baptismal study, Sally was made to choose between Heaven (becoming a member) and Hell (not becoming a member).
- Quotas are set for how many people each member must "reach out to" and bring to activities. Members feel guilty if they don't reach their quota. (Mary, Sally, David)
- Nina was told that she was putting her relationship with Joshua before her obedience to the church.
- Only participation in the activities the group promotes is "seeking first the Kingdom of God." To pursue any other activity is considered not pleasing God or serving Him. As a result, outside activities and interests are dropped, and career goals change to "Kingdom goals." (Michael, Shalon)
- Some members are rebaptized over and over. There is, in fact, a membership form with blanks for Baptism/Re-baptism/Boston Re-baptism/Placed Membership. (Michael)
- "And a lot of people have asked questions, 'Well, why have some of the sisters been re-baptized?' Let me tell you something. No one has been re-baptized around here.

220

Not a single person has been re-baptized around here. I only believe in one baptism." (Kip McKean, "Be Perfectly United")
 • Faults and individual quirks need to be weeded out in members—uniformity is unity. (Michael)
 • To disobey one's discipler is to sin. (Michael)

Cult of Confession
The theme of confession is closely related to the demand for purity. There is an obsession with personal confession, carried beyond any ordinary religious, legal, or therapeutic expression. Rather than focusing on healing, cultic confession becomes a tool of manipulation and exploitation. Information about each member is discussed among leaders.

Confession becomes a means of maintaining a perpetual inner emptying or psychological purge of impurity, which enhances the leadership's hold on the members' guilt feelings. It is a means of maintaining an atmosphere of total exposure—a policy of making known to the organization everything possible about each individual's life experiences, thoughts, and passions, and especially those elements that might be regarded as derogatory or nonconformist.

Confessions contain varying mixtures of revelation and concealment. As Albert Camus observed, "Authors of confessions write especially to avoid confession, to tell nothing of what they know" (quoted in Lifton, 1989, p. 426). When confessing the sins of their precult lives, cult members may leave out ideas and feelings that they are not aware of or are reluctant to discuss, including a continuing identification with their former life. Members may suppress ideas in order to prevent their becoming known to leadership (such ideas may cause persons to be reprimanded or rebuked or to be held back in their advancement in the group).

Confession makes it virtually impossible to attain a reasonable balance between worth and humility. The enthusiastic confessor becomes like Camus's character whose perpetual confession is his means of judging others: "[I] ... practice the profession of penitent to be able to end up as a judge ... the more I accuse myself, the more I have a right to judge you" (Lifton, 1989, p. 427) The individual then is compelled to take on some of the group's arrogance and sense of omnipotence.

Examples

• Members must "seek advice" from their disciplers and be totally open to them, which includes confessing doubts, criticisms, attitudes, and all sins. (David, Mary, Nina, Michael)

• When an individual is constantly confessing and trying to change herself or himself and "die to sin," it is easy to become a judge of other members' behavior. Mary relates that she learned to judge others, as well as herself, as though she were Jesus.

• Disciplers and/or leaders openly discuss the sins and struggles of members so they can learn how to deal with the individual. (Sally, Michael, David)

• After going on dates, members are taught to confess lustful thoughts to their leaders.

• Members confess and apologize to a family group or college ministry. (Michael, James)

• Michael occasionally kept some secrets from his discipler, but was asked very pointed questions until the secrets were revealed.

• An individual is required to confess all sins ever committed before baptism. (Michael, Shalon)

- "Sinful nature: Suggest to the individual with whom you are studying that he or she write a description of their sinful nature and then be specific about various sins they have committed." (*First Principles,* a publication of International Churches of Christ, Pre-baptism study)
- When Shalon confessed that earlier in the week she had felt attracted to someone outside the church, she was told it was a bigger sin because she had not confessed the sin earlier.
- Shalon had to confess that while on vacation she had had some sexual thoughts about some guys on the beach. She was told that Jesus died because Shalon was sexually immoral, that Shalon nailed him to the cross, that Shalon was a murderer.

Sacred Science

The organization maintains an aura of sacredness around its ideology or doctrine, holding it out as an ultimate moral vision for the ordering of human existence. This sacredness is evident in the prohibition (explicit or not) against the questioning of basic assumptions, and in the reverence demanded for the originators of the doctrine, the leaders, and the doctrine itself.

The group's beliefs become an ultimate science, and the person who dares to criticize it or harbor even unspoken alternative ideas becomes not only immoral and irreverent but also "unscientific." The claim of being scientific (having ultimate truth) is needed to gain plausibility and influence in the modern age. A cult combines dogmatic principles (religious, political, scientific, or otherwise) with its claim to special knowledge of human behavior and psychology.

The sacred science can achieve such a strong hold over an individual's mental processes that if the person begins to feel attracted to ideas that either contradict or ignore it, he or she may become guilty and fearful. The individual's quest for knowledge is consequently hampered.

Examples

- The group convinces converts that the Bible cannot be interpreted. Then they give the only "right" interpretation. (Edgar, Michael, James)
- "There is no private interpretation of the Bible." (*First Principles,* pre-baptismal study)
- Members are convinced they must follow the word of God as it is written and have total trust in their leaders as having been chosen by God. When those leaders quote scripture (often out of context and without considering other pertinent scripture that would make the passage more clear) in order to justify a behavior or belief that the member should be following, it becomes impossible for the member to dispute. The Truth has been established and cannot be challenged. (all)
- Members' commitment to the movement becomes synonymous with their commitment to God—blurring the boundaries between the movement, its leaders, and God. (all)
- The doctrine has to be absolutely true and right because "we only follow the Bible." Members are unable to determine the difference between the Bible and man-made rules. If a member questions, she or he is made to feel disobedient to God, disloyal, untrusting, and, therefore, guilty. (all)
- If members do not understand something, they are told to go home and "study it out and pray about it." But

when this is said, it causes members to think that it's their attitude that needs to be changed. Also, when they read appropriate scriptures to "study it out," they read them as taught and interpreted by the group. (David)

• "Exact obedience is thorough and immediate. If we are sloppy or procrastinate in carrying out instructions, we are not obeying as Jesus did. Jesus was obedient because He had a humble, submissive heart. Pride prevents us from being exactly obedient. Pride will cause us to squirm and resist being told what to do and how to do it. Our discipler does not need to prove herself to us ... the accuracy and promptness of our obedience is a barometer of our humility and Christ-likeness." (Robin Deal, "Follow Me," BCC bulletin, Sept. 25, 1988)

"We're all in the Lord and we're all under the authority of the Lord and we're all under authority of our leaders. Whoever disciples us in the Lord." (Kip McKean, "The Dream—Super Churches," 1992)

"When we are under authority, we are to submit and obey our leaders even when they are not very Christ-like." (Al Baird, "Authority and Submission," Part VII)

"The evangelist without elders in the congregation is the authority **of God** in the congregation. The only time he is not to be obeyed is when he calls you to disobey Scripture or disobey your conscience and even **if he calls you to do something that disobeys your conscience, you still have an obligation to study it out and prayerfully change your opinion** so you can be totally unified." (Kip McKean, "Why Do You Resist the Spirit?")

• The ultimate vision of the movement is to evangelize the world by the year 2000. (Refer to quotes from the Evangelization Proclamation)

• As long as members conform in behavior and belief, they have a community, love and acceptance, and a mission or higher purpose. It becomes threatening to entertain thoughts that would cause a disturbance to individual security within this system. If members do not conform, they are challenged, then rebuked, and acceptance and love are withheld.

Loading the Language
A simplified, cliché-ridden language can exert enormous psychological influence, reducing every issue in a complicated life to a single set of slogans that are said to embody the truth as a totality. These terms often become either "god terms" or "devil terms," either very positive (those within the cult mind-set) or very negative (those from the outside world, the unsaved, the unenlightened).

The use of jargon in cults exceeds the boundaries of jargon used in a cultural or organizational group, since cult jargon expresses the claimed certitudes of the sacred science. This loaded language becomes the start and finish of any ideological analysis and prevents members from expressing themselves outside of the group's logic and mind-set.

Examples
• Specific labels are used to describe the progress a potential convert is making: back burner, front burner, crock pot, in the oven, microwave.
• Common jargon used by the Boston movement:

fruit: new converts. A person is fruitful when she or he has brought in new members.

be open: be open to learning from leaders; be open with your life by confessing your doubts, sins, and weakness; be open to correction.

bad attitude: questioning or objecting to advice or correction.

disciple: one fully committed to the group and all its teachings and who has a discipler.

study it out: members are told to do this usually when they have not come to the same conclusion as their leaders or if they have a question.

cranking: going all out to bring guests.

Satan is getting a foothold: spending too much time with people outside the movement.

fell away: left the movement.

sentimentality: a negative term; allowing your relationships with spouses, family, parents to be too important.

Christian: the same as a disciple. Only those in the movement are considered Christians because they are the only ones who have disciples/disciplers.

worldly: outside the movement.

spiritual pornography: critical information about the movement and information about thought reform.

disciple's heart: willing to learn, willing to be submissive, willing to obey.

discipling partner: discipler, one over you in the Lord from whom you must seek advice and to whom you must confess.

reconstruction: a process of assessing the commitment level of a church or member; a "reconstructed church" is a church which has gone through the process.

planting: starting a new church; a "planting" is a new church that has been started by a movement church rather than "reconstructed."

blitzing: going out in a group to canvas an area for the purpose of inviting people to church/Bible Talk/group activities.

227

Quiet Time: mandatory time spent reading the Bible and praying each morning.

probe: what is done by the discipler if the disciple is not open and not confessing; asking critical questions to get at secrets that are being withheld.

awesome brother/sister: really spiritual, will move up in the movement fast.

seek advice: go to your discipler about a decision to be made or about a sin.

marking: to "mark" or name a person as divisive or as an agent of Satan. Members are to have nothing to do with a marked person.

filter: to redefine in your own terms something you were told to do or rebuked for doing by leadership.

Prime Time: in the South Florida Church of Christ, the ministry for reaching out to older people.

Doctrine over Person

This principle is invoked when individual cult members sense a conflict between what they are experiencing and what the group doctrine says they should experience. The cult's message, which gets internalized by the member, is that personal experiences must be negated on behalf of the "truth" found in the cult's dogma. As a result, contradictions one might perceive become associated with guilt, and having doubts becomes an indicator of a person's own deficiency or evil.

The same doctrinal primacy prevails in the totalist approach to changing people. There is a demand that character and identity be reshaped, not in accordance with an individual's special nature or potentialities, but rather to fit 1 the rigid contours of the doctrinal mold.

Examples
- Members must be happy Christians to be able to bring others in. If a member is not joyful and happy, there is something wrong in his or her relationship with God—perhaps unconfessed sin. (David, Mary)
- In order to fulfill all the group requirements and go to all activities, members must get less sleep, often skip meals, neglect studies or work responsibilities as well as families. The activities of the group are considered "seeking first the Kingdom of God." Therefore, movement activities are more important than the needs of the individual. (David, Mary, James, Michael, Shalon)
- Members find themselves denying their unhappiness or depression—even to themselves. (David, Mary)
- Mary was told: "You are being prideful and it is clear in the scriptures that God opposes the proud." Mary couldn't see that she was being prideful, but she could not dispute the leaders.
- Members change life goals and drop outside interests and talents because they need to "seek first the Kingdom"; other things are unimportant, only the goals of the group (God) are important. (David, James)
- Members are pressured to give more and more money, regardless of their financial circumstances. (Edgar, Michael, Shalon)
- In a church service, while singing a serious hymn about Jesus' death on the cross for all of us, Shalon felt introspective and sad but was admonished that the song must be sung with smiles of joy. Shalon became confused and angry.
- The group focuses more on its own growth than on looking after members' problems and needs. (Michael)

229

Dispensing of Existence

Those who have not seen the light and embraced the truth of the group are evil, tainted, unenlightened, and therefore, in some sense (usually metaphorical), lack the right to exist. Participation in the group process is the means by which nonpeople (nonmembers) are permitted, through a change in attitude and personal character, to make themselves over into people (join the group).

Implicit in the dispensing of existence is that cult members feel extremely threatened by any ideas they might have of leaving the group, for they would then become part of the evil, unsaved, outside world. A fear of leaving the group is induced in cult members. To leave the environment means facing the fear of losing what members believe they possess: salvation, enlightenment, perhaps even physical health and psychological well-being.

Examples

• If you leave this church, you are leaving God. (David, Mary, Edgar, Michael)

• "When you walk away from the church of the New Testament, you are walking away from God!" (Al Baird, "Everything You Wanted to Know About the Boston Church of Christ") Note: The movement believes it is *the church* of the New Testament, the only one teaching discipling.

"We believe that those who have left here have left the church. They've left the Lord. And we believe that the Church of Christ in general does not preach, does not teach, does not believe in—as a matter of fact, opposes—the doctrine of making disciples before baptism. And because of that, the vast majority of people in the Church of Christ are not saved." (Joe Garmon, speech during a House Church reconstruction)

- Members are told that people who left the movement turned back to sin. (David)
- "Pat Gempel did a study in which she determined that 90% of the single women who have fallen away were directly or indirectly involved in immorality at the time." (Jake Jensen, "Danger Ahead," BCC bulletin, Oct. 2, 1988)
- Shalon was told by a leader that in leaving the group she was committing spiritual suicide.
- It was Mary's job to warn her niece of the consequences should she leave the church.
- By describing in detail what it feels like to get burned on a stove, Mary could give her niece a better idea of what it would be like in Hell. Should she leave, according to the group, naturally she would go to Hell.
- Mary was led to accept the idea that her husband was on a fast train to Hell because he was not part of the group.
- Members are warned not to talk to people who leave. (Edgar, Sally, Nina)
- Members are convinced that those people who are not members are going to Hell and need to become members. (Sally, Nina, Michael)
- Members are often convinced that the people they loved (nonmembers) who had died went to Hell. (Nina)
- If there is no movement-affiliated church in an area, there is no Christian church there! (Michael)
- All other churches are spiritually dead. (Michael)

Comments

When exposed to thought-reform techniques, individuals are taken through an intense identity crisis. A person's view of reality prior to joining the group is systematically attacked.

This includes a person's view of himself, family, friends, and society as a whole. A person's self-image and ideas about her or his role in life—even who one is in relation to others (such as mother, wife, child, Christian, Jew, sibling)—are called seriously into question. Whatever the person used to think about himself is not right or true any longer. The individual feels fragmented, as though falling apart.

After the group systematically undermines the individual's identity and causes the anxiety of an identity crisis, the leader/group offers the saving ideology. At this point, to resolve the crisis and relieve the pain of loss of identity, the member accepts and adapts to the ideology. The group becomes the cohesive glue to hold the individual self together.

When and if a person leaves the group permanently, with or without exit counseling, she or he faces another identity crisis: what I became inside the group is not real either—so who am I? People who have been exit counseled or who have pursued self-education about cults learn about thought reform. Therefore, they have the tools to begin to sort through their experiences in order to discover what they came to believe and how they came to behave because of the techniques used by the group.

People coming out of cults generally need a lot of support until they can sort through their experiences and attitudes and integrate the group experience into other life experiences outside the group. Some former members may have a difficult time recognizing the negative impact of the experience on their life, yet they may feel "stuck" or unable to get on with life. For this reason, I recommend for further reading:

Critical Perspectives

Captive Hearts, Captive Minds: Freedom and Recovery from Cults and Abusive Relationships by Madeleine Landau Tobias and Janja Lalich (Alameda, CA: Hunter House, 1994).

Cults in Our Midst: The Hidden Menace in Our Everyday Lives by Margaret Thaler Singer with Janja Lalich (San Francisco: Jossey-Bass, 1995).

Influence by Robert Cialdini (Glenview, IL: Scott, Foresman, 1985).

Recovery from Cults: Help for Victims of Psychological and Spiritual Abuse, edited by Michael D. Langone (New York: W. W. Norton, 1993).

During this sorting-out process, former members can also assess what may be valid and positive about their cult experience. There are many positive things people can learn about themselves as a result of having been in a cult or intense group experience. I encourage people who have left such groups to retain the positive aspects and add them to the totality of their life.

References

Robert J. Lifton. Cult formation. *Harvard Mental Health Newsletter,* 1991 (Feb.), pp. 5–7.

Robert J. Lifton. *Thought Reform and the Psychology of Totalism.* Chapel Hill: University of North Carolina Press, 1989.

Margaret Thaler Singer with Janja Lalich. *Cults in Our Midst: The Hidden Menace in Our Everyday Lives.* San Francisco: Jossey-Bass, 1995.

Appendices

Appendix A

Margaret Thaler Singer's Six Conditions for a Thought-Reform Environment[*]

1. Keep the person unaware of what is going on and how she or he is being changed a step at a time.
Potential new members are led, step by step, through a behavioral-change program without being aware of the final agenda or full content of the group. The goal may be to make them deployable agents for the leadership, to get them to buy more courses, or get them to make a deeper commitment, depending on the leader's aims and desires.

2. Control the person's social and/or physical environment; especially control the person's time.
Through various methods, newer members are kept busy and led to think about the group and its content during as much of their waking time as possible.

3. Systematically create a sense of powerlessness in the person.
This is accomplished by getting members away from their normal social support group for a period of time and into an environment where the majority of people are already group

---

[*] These six conditions are based on material presented in *Cults in Our Midst: The Hidden Menace in Our Everyday Lives* by Margaret Thaler Singer with Janja Lalich (Jossey-Bass, 1995).

members. The members serve as models of the attitudes and behaviors of the group and speak an in-group language.

4. Manipulate a system of rewards, punishments, and experiences in such a way as to inhibit behavior that reflects the person's former social identity.
Manipulation of experiences can be accomplished through various methods of trance induction, including leaders' use of such techniques as paced speaking patterns, guided imagery, chanting, long prayer sessions or lectures, and lengthy meditation sessions.

5. Manipulate a system of rewards, punishments, and experiences in order to promote learning the group's ideology or belief system and group-approved behaviors.
Good behavior, demonstrating an understanding and acceptance of the group's ideology, and compliance are rewarded, while questioning, expressing doubts, or criticizing are met with disapproval, redress, and possible rejection. If members ask a question, they are made to feel that there is something inherently wrong with them to be questioning.

6. Put forth a closed system of logic and an authoritarian structure that permits no feedback and refuses to be modified except by leadership approval or executive order.
The group has a top-down, pyramid structure. The leaders must have verbal ways of never losing.

Appendix B

Robert Lifton's Eight Psychological Themes[*]

1. Milieu Control
This involves the control of information and communication within the environment and, ultimately, within the individual, resulting in a significant degree of isolation from society at large.

2. Mystical Manipulation
Experiences are manipulated to appear spontaneous but in fact are planned and orchestrated by the group or its leaders to "demonstrate" divine authority, spiritual advancement, or some special gift or talent, which then allows the leaders to reinterpret events, scriptures, and experiences as they please.

3. Demand for Purity
The world is viewed as black and white and members are constantly exhorted to conform to the ideology of the group and strive for perfection. The induction of guilt and/or shame is a powerful control device used here.

4. Confession
Sins, as defined by the group, are to be confessed either to a personal monitor or publicly to the group. There is no

---

[*] This is based on *Thought Reform and the Psychology of Totalism* by Robert Jay Lifton, chap. 22 (University of North Carolina Press, 1989).

confidentiality; members' "sins," "bad attitudes," and "faults" are discussed and exploited by the leaders.

5. Sacred Science
The group's doctrine or ideology is considered to be the ultimate Truth, beyond all questioning or dispute. Truth is not to be found outside the group. The leader, as the spokesperson for God or for all humanity, is likewise above criticism.

6. Loading the Language
The group interprets or uses words and phrases in new ways so that often the outside world does not understand. This jargon consists of thought-terminating clichés which serve to alter members' thought processes to conform to the group's way of thinking.

7. Doctrine over Person
Members' personal experiences are subordinated to the sacred science and any contrary experiences must be denied or reinterpreted to fit the ideology of the group.

8. Dispensing of Existence
The group has the prerogative to decide who has the right to exist and who does not. This is usually not literal but means that those in the outside world are not saved, are unenlightened or unconscious, and must be converted to the group's ideology. If they do not join or are critical of the group, then they must be rejected by the members. Thus, the outside world loses all credibility. Similarly, members who leave the group must be rejected also.

About the Editors

Carol Giambalvo is a former member of est and the Hunger Project. She has been an exit counselor since 1984, and is a cofounder of reFOCUS, a national support network for former cult members. She is on AFF's board of directors and is responsible for its Project Outreach. Author of *Exit Counseling: A Family Intervention* (AFF, 1995), Ms. Giambalvo has written and lectured extensively on cult-related topics.

Herbert L. Rosedale, Esq., is a senior partner at a New York City law firm. He is president of AFF, a nonprofit institute focusing on cult research and education. He has been involved in cult education and cult-related litigation for fifteen years, and is author of several articles on the subject. He is also author of "Legal Considerations: Regaining Independence and Initiative," a chapter in *Recovery from Cults: Help for Victims of Psychological and Spiritual Abuse,* edited by M.D. Langone (W.W. Norton, 1993).

About the Contributors

James Ash (a pseudonym) tells his story in chapter 4.

Nina Cuong (a pseudonym) tells her story in chapter 6.

Lorna Goldberg, M.S.W., L.C.S.W., is a faculty member of the New Jersey Institute for Psychoanalysis. With her husband, William, she has conducted a support group for former cult members for eighteen years, and also works with ex-cult members in psychotherapy. She is also author of "Guidelines for Therapists," a chapter in *Recovery from Cults: Help for Victims of Psychological and Spiritual Abuse,* edited by M. Langone (W.W. Norton).

William Goldberg, M.S.W., L.C.S.W., is the director of the Community Support Center in Pomona, New York. With his wife, Lorna, he has conducted a former cult members support group for eighteen years. He also does individual counseling with ex-cult members. He is also author of "Guidelines for Support Groups," a chapter in *Recovery from Cults: Help for Victims of Psychological and Spiritual Abuse,* edited by M. Langone (W.W. Norton).

Shalon Goldsby, a former member of the San Francisco Church of Christ, is a senior at the University of California, Berkeley. She has aspirations of being a teacher and a writer.

Critical Perspectives

Kimberly Logan (a pseudonym) is director of a local support group for families and ex-cult members. She has been active in educating the public about destructive groups. Recently she organized a regional seminar on cults, and also worked with a television station on a special report on the International Churches of Christ.

Mary Sartorio, a former member of the New York City Church of Christ, is a middle school math teacher with a master's degree in applied mathematics. She has lectured about her experiences, and has appeared on two television shows about the Boston movement.

Robert Watts Thornburg has been Dean of Marsh Chapel and chaplain to the University at Boston University since 1978, where he works with nine other University chaplains in the spiritual nurture of 27,000 students. The first campus appearance of the Boston Church of Christ was at Marsh Chapel in November of 1979, and Dean Thornburg has been following the group since that time.

Michael West, a former member of the Central Nashville Church of Christ, graduated from Vanderbilt University. He teaches and counsels adolescent psychiatric inpatients at Middle Tennessee Mental Health Institute in Nashville. He is working toward a master's degree in psychology.

Edgar Vann (a pseudonym) tells his story in chapter 7.

Sally Young (a pseudonym) tells her story in chapter 5.

About the Publisher

AFF (formerly known as the American Family Foundation) is a secular, nonprofit, tax-exempt research center and educational organization founded in 1979. AFF's mission is to study manipulation and cultic groups, to educate the public and professionals, and to assist those who have been adversely affected by a cult experience.

AFF consists of a professional staff and a growing network of more than one hundred volunteer professionals in fields ranging from education, psychology, and religion to journalism, law, law-enforcement, and business. AFF is funded by grants, literature sales, and donations.

For more information, write or call

AFF
P.O. Box 2265
Bonita Springs, FL 33959
Tel: (212) 533-5420
Message Center: (212) 249-7693